I Want More

I Want More

Straight-talking advice on how to get what you want

STEPHANIE MYERS

Thorsons
An Imprint of HarperCollins*Publishers*

Thorsons
An Imprint of HarperCollins*Publishers*
77–85 Fulham Palace Road,
Hammersmith, London W6 8JB
1160 Battery Street,
San Francisco, California 94111–1213

Published by Thorsons 1995
1 3 5 7 9 10 8 6 4 2

A catalogue record for this book is available from the British Library

ISBN 0 7225 3186 9

Printed in Great Britain by HarperCollinsManufacturing Glasgow

This book is dedicated with love to my mother, who
taught us by example that we can do anything if
we're determined.

To my family whose total support has given me
the courage to make mistakes.

To Sharmaine, Eve, Kathryn, Mandy R & Mandy
B. I know I'm lucky to have friends like you.

And to all those who will never know just how much
they helped and inspired me, especially Jung,
Orlando, Donald and Elsa.

Last, but definitely not least, this book is dedicated to
you, the reader. In buying this book, you have helped
a fellow citizen to regain their self respect.

Thank you all.

Contents

Introduction

I moved to London because I was offered a job with a multi-national company, which was willing to pay me a large sum of money. One winter's morning, walking from the tube station to the office, I passed a young person in a doorway. He was wrapped in a thin blanket which was covered in a layer of snow. I cried at the thought that in one of the greatest cities of the world, we all allowed this to happen.

It's taken me a few years to figure out how I could do more than occasionally give away spare change. I want to sell 100,000 copies of *I Want More*, and thus donate £20,000 to help the homeless. (Unfortunately, I only get 36p per book sold.) With your help, we're now one step closer to the goal.

There is another reason for writing this book – everywhere I go, I see people who are frustrated, fed up, and unhappy. I call them the forgotten majority. Nobody thinks they deserve any special attention, and no one bothers to tell them the secrets to living happier, more successful lives.

This book won't make you into a millionaire or find you that ideal partner, but it will help you to see where you might have been going wrong, and what you can do about it. It aims to show you above all else, that you're *not* powerless.

I Want More will provide the answers to some of the questions which have been dogging us for years: Why haven't we been promoted? Why does everyone take us for granted? How can we get more love and fun from our relationships? How can we make more money when we're in a dead end job?

This is no ordinary book. Be prepared for some straight talking and total honesty.

Read and enjoy!

I Want More . . . Love

The only way to have a friend is to be one

RALPH EMERSON (1803–82)

The Beatles told us decades ago that money can't buy us love, yet every year we spend billions on whatever the advertizers tell us will help. We buy sexy clothes, we study magazines looking for answers, we join certain clubs, we watch films with happy endings and try to see what tips we can pick up.

Often, when we think we are looking for love, what we really want is companionship. We want someone who we can share things with, who will spoil us, and tell us how great we are. Someone, in short, who will make us feel good. Those of us who have partners don't believe we're loved enough, and those without think that's the root of our problems. We want partners who are more patient/considerate/feminine/macho/sensitive/spontaneous or demonstrative. What we're talking about here is romantic love – the sort that Hollywood and the media have told us is more important than any other. We're encouraged to take for granted all other forms of love, no matter how unselfish and pure. But there *are* other forms of love we must consider:

Forgotten Forms of Love

Anyone whose mother is still alive, is loved unconditionally. Why is it then, that we all say 'yes, but that's not enough'? Mums always make us feel good about ourselves, they forgive us when we've done something we're ashamed of, and never ask for anything more than an occasional phonecall or visit. The trouble is, you can't usually go on an all-night session with your mum, or go to a party with her. She's a different generation, and so sees the world through 'old fashioned' eyes. That's where friends come in.

A true friend is one who knows the worst about us, and loves us just the same. Friends are like mums of our own age. They support even our wildest schemes, lend us their best clothes, always agree to get drunk with us when we're down, and don't mind us waking them up in the middle of the night. They share our passion for football, shopping, trainspotting and chocolate. In some ways, they're even better than mothers, because we never feel the need to tidy up or wear something respectable when they visit. They won't judge us if there's nothing in the fridge except beer and they'll never tell us it's time we settled down.

Although I'm on shaky ground here, we can't talk about love without mentioning children, can we? I don't have any of my own, so I've watched other people's, and thought about how I behave with nephews and nieces. One thing's for sure – kids have mega amounts of love to give, and aren't afraid to show it.

Hands up all those who only love their kids when they get presents from them, or who only believe their kids love them if they say it every day. (Bear with me, sometimes we have to look at the extreme to make something sink in.) In theory then, as long as we have a mother, a few friends and access to kids, we should be happy. But we're not.

The Missing Ingredients

So let's get down to what it is that we can't get from friends and family. For a start, sex. Somehow it doesn't mean as much when mum says 'You look lovely, dear' as it does when a person you're attracted to says 'Wow!'.

Second, friends and family have this annoying habit of just assuming we know they love us, so they rarely bother to say it. Instead they quite rightly conclude that actions speak louder than words.

But because we've been brought up to believe that if someone loves us, they have to tell us *constantly*, we long for a partner who's willing to say it while we're brushing our teeth, farting in front of the telly, wearing a face mask, or hanging wallpaper. If this was a natural state of affairs, wouldn't our mates and mothers be saying it every time they saw us?

Insecurity

The truth of the matter is, the more insecure we feel about a person, the more we want to be told that they love us. And why are we so insecure? Because we expect our lovers to want no one but us – to love us unconditionally like our mothers do.

Regardless of how fantastic we might think we are, we also have difficulty believing that we really are the best lover on this planet, and so are always worried that our partners will someday decide to leave us for someone who *does* put the top back on the toothpaste/*likes* wearing leather knickers/doesn't have a beer gut or cellulite/likes football, or even someone who their mother likes.

What we mean then, when we say we want love (or more love), is that we want *one person* to satisfy all of our emotional needs: a partner who is a friend (i.e. who will always be there for us, and always a good laugh), who thinks of us as a mother (i.e. they only have the one, and she's the best on earth), who finds us sexy first thing in the morning, and who also happens to worship us like a god (constant sacrifices/presents, and declaring their undying love).

Let's take the friendship angle first: if we expected our friends to constantly buy us presents, phone us at work to say they loved us and generally feed our egos, they'd soon be so worn down, they'd walk away for good. Our friendships are special because we *don't* feel the need to state the obvious twenty times a day. i.e. that we think our mates are wonderful human beings.

OK, let's try mothers: imagine if our mothers phoned us at work every day to tell us they loved us – we'd feel totally stifled and secretly wish that they'd hurry up and get a life. If they constantly bought us presents, wouldn't we be quick to tell them that they shouldn't waste their money on us? I doubt we'd take the presents into work as some sort of trophy and show off to our colleagues about how much our mums loved us.

Yet we all at some stage have wanted to boast about the gifts from our partners. It's like we need to reassure ourselves as well as outsiders that they really love us. As for conditional love – 'If you loved me you'd . . . have sex with me/drop your friends/never get drunk/do the housework/buy me a car/move in with me/give me space' – Get Real!

We all know how great it is when someone finds us attractive, yet even this leads to problems. If they say they love our eyes, we get nervous every time we see anyone with a decent set of peepers. If we tell them we love their muscley legs, they stick to us like glue every time a jogger approaches.

Finally, let's look at the godlike worship: if they never buy us presents it's because they're inconsiderate, whereas when they do it's 'obvious' that they're feeling guilty about something. When we buy them presents, it's because we're trying to change them. Then we expect them to spend the rest of their lives raving about how much they liked it.

Breaking Up

Every time we have a failed love affair, we promise ourselves, as we look through the bottom of a glass or break off another chunk of chocolate, that we'll never make the same mistakes again. The problem is, we don't really understand what the mistakes were. Was it the dirty socks on the floor, the nagging, the all-night drinking sessions, the lateness, the impotency, the frigidity, the addiction to soap operas, or the one-night stand?

Usually, it's none of these. (Don't get me wrong, all of them are a pain in the ass in their own right.) It's something much deeper, much more fundamental. But it's easier to blame something petty (no one really leaves their partner over toothpaste caps/leaving the toilet seat up) or to simply lie: when someone says they're not ready for commitment, they only mean not with *you*. How many of us have an ex who seemed to get married before we'd even had time to change the locks?

Few of us are rational and fair when a relationship ends –
we either blame ourselves or damn the bitch/bastard to hell.
Neither of these responses is particularly constructive. In the
first instance, our self-esteem is damaged to such an extent
that when we next go out with someone, we let them treat us
like shit; and in the second case, we're so determined not to let
anyone hurt us again, that we treat *them* like shit. (This is
why, when you meet someone whose previous relationship
has recently ended, you must ask them not to call you for
three months.)

Never Learning From The Past

However, hope eventually triumphs over experience, and
before long we're on the look-out again for that ideal partner.
The older we are, the lower our self- esteem, or the more failed
relationships we've had, the more desperate we become. And
so, if need be, we lower our expectations to the point where
we make allowances for bad breath/embarrassing dress
sense/Neanderthal personality/lack of excitement and even
lack of anything in common.

Many of us then condemn ourselves to lives of quiet desperation, trying to make do with what we have, while secretly
believing there must be more. (Hence we buy books like this,
get drunk more regularly, lose ourselves in our work, or have
affairs.) Depending on how much we worry about what other
people think of us, and whether we have another bed to climb
into, we may eventually leave.

The trouble is the whole process will simply start again,
because we have never taken the time, or had the courage to

really look at what the problem is.

The Root Of All Heartache

In 99% of cases, the fundamental problem is that we don't love ourselves. (Often we don't even particularly *like* ourselves.) The reason this is a problem is that if we don't really love ourselves, we don't believe that anyone else could.

Even when all evidence suggests otherwise (i.e. we have family and mates who think we're something special), we dismiss it by saying things like 'But she's my mother, it's her job to love me' or 'we're not really close mates, we just both like football/shopping/drinking', or even, 'Yeah, but they don't count'.

People who don't love themselves spend their lives playing victim. Things happen to them, nothing's their fault, they envy everyone, but won't accept that they've *chosen* the lives they have (however sad and pathetic those lives may be). They measure happiness in material and external terms – with the right car/ house/income/clothes or partner they expect to gain friends, status and happiness.

This isn't to say that wanting big bucks in your bank account means you don't love yourself. What I'm saying is that if we can't say for sure that our friends, family and partners would still be around if we had nothing more than the clothes we stood up in, we're self-haters.

If the thought of losing our wealth is more terrifying than the thought of losing those we love, it's time to take stock. If we stay with a partner who is violent, unfaithful or just plain selfish, we're committing suicide. (It doesn't take a razor blade or bottle of pills to show the world that we hate our lives, or that we have no self-respect.)

What we need to remember is that people take their cue for how to treat us by watching how we treat ourselves. So if we're always putting ourselves down, or only ever talk about money, they'll put us down as well, or think that money is more important to us than love and affection.

When I'm Loving, They're Loving

So what does loving ourselves actually involve? It's doing everything for ourselves that we would for our ideal partner, whether that means buying ourselves expensive presents, forgiving ourselves when we do something we're not proud of, accepting that we're not perfect, focusing on the things we really like about ourselves, or making an effort to look nice. When we love ourselves, just as when we're in love with someone else, nothing is as important as our happiness.

Although it's wonderful to be in love, and to be loved by others, one of the best-kept secrets is that we attract loving people by first being loving. If sensitivity and kindness are what we seek, what are the chances of attracting these when we're harassing women in bars, or cutting people dead with our razor-sharp wit? When we seek fidelity and security, it makes little sense to chase a person who has a different partner for each day of the week.

By the same token, people are hardly likely to respect a doormat, buy presents for a miser, dress up for a slob, invite a beer monster to parties, take a soap freak to the theatre, or plan surprises for someone whose middle name is Predictability.

There are a million ways to attract more love. What they all

have in common is that we must always start by loving ourselves first. So let's look at some practical steps we can take
which don't involve too much pain or hard work. They *will*
require some action, so get a pen and start now. This is not a
novel, it's an education!

LOVING OURSELVES

1) List 6 of your best personality traits – the things your family
and friends like most about you.

....

....

....

....

....

....

2) List 6 things which make you feel good.

....

....

....

....

....

....

3) List at least 6 people who enjoy being with you.

....

....

....

....

....

....

Right, well that wasn't so hard was it? Hopefully, from this short exercise, you'll realise that all is not lost. Assuming you managed to answer all three questions, there *is* hope: you have a decent personality, people who like you, and you know what it takes to make you feel good. All we have to do now is use your answers to these for your action plan. (See, you're not going to get very far if you thought you'd skip the homework and catch up later, are you? Go back and do it now, we'll wait for you.)

Hey, I'm A Nice Person!

To break you in gently, I've made the first step easy: all you have to do is think of an unselfish thing you did for someone else, whether it was walking their dog, saving their lives, or paying them a compliment. Try to remember how you felt, and how they reacted.

Although we're all pretty nice, loveable people, we occasionally need to remind ourselves just how yummy we are. The knack is to try to keep in mind lots of pleasant and kind things we've done in the past, with no ulterior motive. The more things we can think of, the more we'll start to actually quite like ourselves.

N.B. This is not intended to be some sort of score sheet, where you keep tabs on how many favours people owe you. If you do that, you'll be back to square one, feeling taken for granted, or some kind of mug. If some people haven't returned your favours, it just means they're not as nice a person as you are.

OK, so we've established that we're vaguely kind and love-able people. That doesn't solve the problem of wanting more love than we're currently getting though does it? I'm just coming on to that – you know you have to eat your greens before you get dessert! Below are 21 tips guaranteed to make you feel more loved, and to attract more (demonstrative) love:

Getting More Love

1) If you don't feel loved by your partner, tell them (calmly), and then suggest at least five things that would help e.g. spending more time together, going out more, the occasional (genuine) compliment.

2) Do as you would be done by – if you love the idea of getting a short phonecall in the middle of the day from your nearest and dearest, phone them, and tell them how much you want them/love them/miss them. Believe me, not only do you make them feel good, and look forward to seeing you, but they'll also start doing the same.

3) Make a deal, if you live with someone, never to go to sleep on an argument. No matter how drunk/angry either of you are, promise each other you'll talk through whatever's wrong. You *know* the best part of arguing is the making up afterwards.

4) Diary note to phone all the relatives who you actually like, at least once a month, wherever they are. The nice thing about these people is that you're under no obligation to them, and they'll always be glad to hear from you.

5) Stop feeling guilty about spending money on yourself. You're worth it.

6) Diary note to do at least three of the things which make you feel good, every month. (If we don't take the time to make ourselves feel good, why should anyone else?)

7) Either set the alarm 10 minutes early, or plan from the night before what you're going to wear. Choose clothes which make you feel attractive. If you don't have any, go shopping with a friend whose dress sense you admire. Although it's true that when we look good, we feel good, this exercise will achieve more than this. When we make an effort, we're making a statement to the world that we believe we're worth spending time on – again, they'll take their cue.

8) Get a life! This may sound harsh, but some of us need a good kick up the backside before we wake up and smell the coffee. The law of averages means that the more people you meet, the more chances you'll have of meeting ones who are loving. Couch potatoes rarely have a crowd of friends or admirers beating a path to their doors, so get out there!

9) Plan to socialize at least once a week (with or without your partner/friends). It's important to choose something that you're interested in, and which will involve meeting and talking to new people. Maybe this could tie in with things which make you feel good e.g. writing poetry (join a group), tinkering with the car (join a mechanics class), singing (amateur dramatics), sport (local team/club), cooking (dinner parties where each friend brings a guest), clothes (volunteer to work in a charity shop). Get the idea? The more imaginative your idea, the more fun it's likely to be.

I'm fully aware that some of you will hesitate because you're shy. Let's make a deal: you pluck up all your courage just once to do something new (knowing that if you don't like it, you can always leave), and if it's not for you, never go back, but if you love it, you'll lend this book to someone else who might benefit. Can't say fairer than that, can I?

10) Be nice to people. Sounds simple, costs nothing, and yet most of us don't even bother. Have you seen the look on a person's face when you pay them a spontaneous compliment? Or noticed the effect a smile can have? The nicer people think you are, the more they'll want you around, and the nicer they'll be to you. A word of advice – be sincere. Don't pay a compliment like you expect a receipt.

11) Become interested in other people – at work, at home, in your social life, everywhere. When you take an interest in what makes other people happy, they'll do the same. You may find that they have similar interests to you, but never mentioned it before because no one ever asked.

12) Be honest – when something or someone annoys or offends you, say so, and when they make you happy, let them know it. Human brains may be more powerful than computers, but few of us are telepathic. Reinforce the behaviour you like, and put a stop to any you don't.

13) Stop playing conditional love games. *Never* start a sentence with 'If you loved me you would. . . ' You *know* in your heart of hearts whether someone loves you or not. If they do, questioning their love will only hurt them, and if they don't, what are you doing with them?

14) Spend time with children (yours or someone else's). If you really don't like kids, a pet is an alternative. If you don't like either, you may as well just brick up your front door, and call it a day, 'cause you're past redemption. Children and animals bring out the best in us, and have no qualms about showing love. All we have to give is a small amount of attention, or show one act of kindness, to be rewarded with smiles/hugs/kisses/tail-wagging or purring. Take a friend's dog for a walk, or kids to the park, and you'll come back exhausted but happy. (Your friend will love you for it too.)

15) Get together with one of the people you listed earlier, and set yourselves a 'Sunday Challenge' – each of you has to come up with three things to do on a specific Sunday, which you think the other will enjoy. (Make sure you choose someone who knows you well; it's hard to explain calmly why bungee-jumping and vertigo don't mix when someone's strapping you in enthusiastically.)

16) Is it just me, or do dating agencies and personal ads smack of desperation? I reckon that in the vast majority of cases, when we go out looking for romance rather than friendship, we're setting ourselves up for disappointment. You know how, when you're on your way out, and a button comes off, you rush around madly searching for a safety pin? And how you never find one until weeks later when you're cleaning the fridge? Well, frantically searching for romance has similar results. When you stop looking, you'll find it in the most unlikely places.

   So chill out, get on with your life, and let it happen naturally. Think about it – would you want to spend time with someone who seemed ready to go down the aisle before they knew your surname?

17) Bring back the child in you. Apart from the few strange people who are now safely bricked up at home, everyone loves kids and occasional childish behaviour. If you're the sort of person who loves getting presents, talk to your lover/friends about which were your favourite sweets/ toys when you were young. Few things compare to the feeling I get when a friend stops off at a shop on their way to see me, and buys me some Jelly Tots.

You may think this is nothing to get excited about, but stop and think what's involved in such a simple act. a) The friend is saying 'hey, I was thinking about you, and wanted to do something to make you happy' so, b) I feel loved by someone who thinks about me when I'm not around and c) because it's a small, inexpensive gift, I don't feel indebted, and they don't feel I'm after their money. I even have a sister who lives 100 miles away, and sends Jelly Tots through the post – beats reading a gas bill first thing in the morning!

18) Wave goodbye to one-night stands and sex on a first date. (Yes, even if Harrison or Whitney beg!) If you don't know someone well enough to trust them with your car/savings/spare key, what are you doing sharing one of your most valuable assets with them?

19) Visit your mum one weekend. (Unless of course, the idea of someone being so pleased to see you that they cook your favourite meals and give you breakfast in bed, doesn't appeal.)

20) Organize a party. You'll be surprised at how many friends there are in your address book that you haven't seen for ages. If money or space are limited, just make it a small affair – anything from a few cans and videos, to chocolate fingers, jelly and ice-cream.

21) One rainy Sunday, when you've nothing to do, send cards/notes to everyone you like, regardless of how long it's been since you last saw them. You don't have to write

more than a line, saying 'Hi, how are things?' or 'Let's go for a drink some time'. Over the following few weeks, you'll feel wonderful about the number of people who call you, write to you, or just pop round out of the blue.

Mortgage Prostitutes

Some of the saddest people I know are mortgage prostitutes: the (usually) women who live in loveless marriages or relationships, and put up with mental, verbal, or even physical abuse from their partners. They know as well as we do that they should leave and start to rebuild their lives, but they don't. Why?

Because in exchange for occasional sex and their self-esteem, they are given a nice house, status (often their social lives are dependent on their partner's work), and enough money to buy nice clothes.

The first time I used the phrase 'Mortgage Prostitutes', I was told it was a bit harsh. But what else do you call someone who exchanges sex and affection for money? The difference between the mortgage prostitute in suburbia, and the 'woman of the streets', is that one does it as a job, which she can walk away from at the end of the day, while the other sacrifices her whole life. It's not for us to make judgements on the rights and wrongs of prostitution. All I want to do is show people how to make their lives more enjoyable and fulfilling.

So what do you do if you are, or you think you're becoming a mortgage prostitute? First, you try to develop a social life of your own, totally separate from your partner's work. Join clubs, gyms or do some voluntary work. You have to start making friends with people who like you for yourself, not just because they're in the same boat as you, or because they're trying to help their partners to get promotion.

Next, you read and re-read the respect and confidence chapters, completing all of the exercises, until the message sinks in. Then try the strengths and skills questionnaire in the job satisfaction chapter, to remind yourself what you're good at.

Following this, either enrol on a course to improve your skills, or start looking for a job. It's time you regained your self-esteem, and some independence. Obviously, these tips are for those who are not happy with their lives. If you're enjoying things the way they are, then who am I to tell you to change? I would just give you one word of warning – if you don't have any outside interests, your partner could become bored with you. And bored partners often stray, to find excitement.

Sour Relationships

Not every couple in an unhappy relationship needs to split up. Often all that's required is a trip down memory lane. Think about it; if your partner fell in love with you because you were ambitious, attractive, sporty, always active, or always thinking up mad things to do, and then after you've been together for a while, all this stops, they're gonna feel cheated and conned.

The trouble is, a lot of people think that once they've 'got the man/woman' they don't have to try any more. Then they wonder why their partners don't treat them as they want to be treated, leave them, or start having affairs.The classic example is when an intelligent career woman, with a busy social life, marries and becomes a housewife. Suddenly, she no longer has any funny or interesting little stories to tell her husband about what happened at work. If her only contribution to a conversation is to say 'I took the kids to school, and cleaned the kitchen', her man is going to feel bored.

Don't misunderstand, I'm not blaming the woman. Often (yes even in the '90s) a man will say that he wants his wife to give up work when they're married, not realising he's destroying a part of her he fell in love with. She then becomes like his mother was when he was a child – always there when he gets home, with a meal on the table.

If you're in a sour relationship, take a few minutes to think about what you were like when your partner fell in love with you. What did they love about you most? What made them laugh when they were with you? Then you have to find a way to bring these things back. It doesn't have to involve going back to work. It might be as simple as planning your week more effectively, so that the two of you go out together twice a week to the same sort of places you used to, or that you lose a few pounds, or get active in your community.

Be honest, are you really as interesting to talk to as you were five years ago? Do you have as many interesting things happen to you in an average day as you used to? If the answer to either question is no, this may be where your problem is.

Often our partners start taking us for granted when we've been in a relationship for a while. The easiest way to put a stop to that is to stop being predictable. Start doing the unexpected. If they expect you to be home every evening while they're out with their mates, arrange a night out with *your* mates. If you always wear dowdy clothes and sit in the corner at parties while they flirt, buy an outfit which will turn heads, and dance your heart out. (With or without them.)

That's our love section over and done with. As you'll probably have realized from many of the suggestions, if you want more, you first have to give more. Unlike many things in this world, there are no limits to the amount of love one person can give or receive: start by giving yourself more, and then share it with others.

Many people have real problems putting their own happiness first. After years of making their parents, partners, children, or bosses a priority they feel guilty and selfish if they stop. My final words must go to them:

Answer the following questions:

1) Would these people love you less if you stopped being a doormat?

2) What does that tell you?

Promise yourself you'll try to use at least some of these tips for one month. Go on, you've got nothing to lose.

To love oneself is the beginning of a life-long romance

OSCAR WILDE (1854–1900)

CHAPTER TWO

I Want More . . . Money

Let me tell you about the very rich
They're different from you & me.

F. SCOTT FITZGERALD (1896–1940)

Yes, they have more money.

ERNEST HEMINGWAY (1898–1961)

Having greed as one of the seven deadly sins is a bit uncomfortable. It seems silly to condemn something we all feel. I think that's why we invented the word ambition. The interesting thing about money is that no one is ever satisfied with the amount they have. The few people I know who have any wealth worth talking about either worry that they'll lose it, or half kill themselves trying to increase it.

How many people do you know who happily admit that they have enough? What about the ones who think they have too much? (Please send their details to the address at the back of this book before reading any further.) Maybe you're the one. Maybe you're just reading this because you're curious to know what poor people do about being broke. We worry, that's what. And when we're sick of worrying, we rebel. e.g. we go on a massive spending spree, or spend frightening amounts on drink. The next day, we realize what we've done, and worry even more than before!

If we're honest, most of us would have to admit that we're not about to starve, and that we do have more than one set of clothes. So it's not that we need more money for survival, it's that we need more money to satisfy our desires. And why not? There must be more to life than work and budgeting, surely?

Rich People Take Risks

To the best of my knowledge, there's no shortage of money in the world overall. It's just that most of it seems to avoid the vast majority of us. So the question on everybody's lips is, 'What are we doing wrong?'. Well for a start, we're playing safe: the really rich people in this world (excluding the royals), are the rock stars, media stars, writers, sports champions, inventors and business owners. They most definitely aren't middle managers living in suburbia. In fact, they are rarely anyone who works for someone else.

If we want to make big bucks, we have to be willing to take risks. The people we all envy are ones who may have started in a factory, shop or office, but at some stage broke free to follow their dreams. Perhaps it would be worth pausing for a moment to remember some of the ways people have made their fortunes in the past :

Walt Disney had the courage to go to Hollywood with his pencil drawing of a mouse, and Colonel Sanders managed to sell a home recipe, so what's stopping us? Les Paterson (Dame Edna Everidge), and Danny La Rue must have had a hard time when they started out. Anita Roddick originally painted her first shop walls green to hide the mould, and was considered a crank for promoting animal-friendly products.

Linford Christie's trainer was ready to resign unless he

made a choice between 100% effort in athletics or dabbling in it along with other interests. As we know, he chose to give up everything else and go for gold. Many thought he'd left it too late to ever become a champion. How many of us have given up because a few negative cling-ons told us we'd never make it? (Cling-ons are the people who drag you down in life, and try to stop you realizing your full potential.)

I remember paying £2 to see Ben Elton perform live, when I was a student seven years ago. The mainstream press thought him too alternative, too shocking and too loud. Last year, he starred in the BBC TV adaptation of one of his books. If he had listened to the critics and reviewers, he'd probably be like most of us are now – bitter and frustrated, because he 'never had a chance' to be successful.

Playing It Safe Is An International Sport

There's a simple fact which we all know, but often forget or ignore: human beings are suspicious of, and frightened of change. We feel safer when everyone does what's expected of them, plays by the rules, and doesn't dare to be different. What's interesting is that we don't have these feelings about new products. We see the benefits in constant improvements and inventions.

But when a banker decides to resign and become a traveller, when a woman says she doesn't want children, when a Harvard graduate decides to be a rock star, or when a man stays at home to look after his kids, we panic.

First, we try to make them 'see sense'. In reality, this means we try to persuade them to play it safe, like us. Next we try ridicule and threats. If we can't make them feel stupid, we 'reason' that they'll become laughing stocks, outcasts and failures. I'll let you into a secret: we're jealous. And this jealousy is what makes us into cling-ons. We don't like to see that someone has more courage than us. In fact, we resent their courage so much, we often hope they fail. At least then we can say 'I told you so', and feel better about playing it safe.

What do I mean by 'playing it safe'? Doing a job we get no satisfaction from, living a frustrated life, where we do what's expected of us, not what we know we'd enjoy. It's a common misconception that the alternative is to be irresponsible or reckless. BULL! ALTHOUGH MAKING MONEY WILL ALWAYS INVOLVE RISK-TAKING, BY MAKING PLANS WE CAN AVOID ANY SERIOUS LOSS.

Planning and Choosing Our Risks

I know you're not convinced, so let me give you some examples: say you have a boring job in an office, and in your spare time, you play a sport, or have a hobby. I'm not saying that you instantly give up your day-time job and try to make money from writing or golf. What I am saying is that if you would really like to spend more time on these activities, you can continue to do your day-time job while you research and improve in your chosen field.

Set yourself a deadline e.g. decide that in three years' time you will save enough money or make contacts with willing investors to start a business. Make a list of all that you need to know, what qualifications you need, the most successful people in the industry, the amount of money required to get started. Work out an action plan, and then get started.

From the moment you commit yourself, there will be two

main benefits: first, your day-time job won't be such a drag, because the money you earn is helping you to get what you really want from life; and second, you'll feel excited about the challenge you've set yourself. (When was the last time you felt really excited about something?)

I'm aware that some of you are thinking that you don't have any hobbies or talents, and anyway, you just about earn enough to pay the bills, so there's no hope of saving. Again I say 'BULL'. There is always something that we like doing which can be turned into a money-making idea. So you think that because you spend most of your time in a bar, or at home with the kids this doesn't apply to you? Wrong again!

If you enjoy being in a bar so much (and I'm assuming that you don't have a drink problem), why not find out what you need to do to run one? Contact the brewers of your favourite beer, and ask them. Talk to the landlord/owner of the bar you go to most often. If you're a regular, you probably have some ideas on how to improve the place. You know what it's like to be a customer, so just list all the best and worst things from a customer's point of view about bars in general, and come up with a way of making yours the best.

Don't dwell on reasons why you *can't*, start thinking of reasons why you will. You can try working in a bar a few nights to see if you like it. If you do, get a job managing someone else's bar while they're on holiday. When you feel you have enough experience and knowledge, then buy or lease your own.

I haven't forgotten you, Mr or Ms parent. You enjoy spending time with your kids? Start a nursery. Make it the sort of place you would take your own kids to, and it'll be popular with all the other parents who need help. Get the qualifications you need, ask all your friends how much they can afford to spend on childcare, contact businesses to see if you can do a deal with them to look after their employees' kids. Find an old disused building, and do it up yourself at weekends. Pick up toys and books from car boot sales. Ask everyone you know with older kids to donate something they don't need any more.

Don't think you could handle anyone else's kids? Write stories for your own. If they like them, chances are, others will too. You don't have to give up the day-time job until you've sold a few.

There's one major group I haven't dealt with yet – the couch potatoes. Those who are at home all day, or who come home from work or college, and just sit in front of the TV until it's time for bed. What's your favourite programme? Soaps? OK start a fanclub – all you need is a newsletter and some juicy information. Write to the stars and tell them what you're trying to do. They should have the sense to realize it could make them more popular, and so will be quite support- ive. They might even invite you on to the set, or arrange to meet you. If you get the programme makers on board, they might agree to either employ you officially, or to promote the newsletter at the end of the show. Been done? Fine, get trained to be a make-up artist, wardrobe assistant or director, and then go freelance. Sports fanatics: why not train as a referee, umpire or even commentator? Why not set up a training school?

All the successful people I've mentioned didn't just wake up one morning and think 'What the hell, I'm gonna risk every- thing today'. They weighed up the situation, and looked at the pros and cons.

The easiest recipe for us to follow is the WPS. This stands for Worst Possible Scenario. Whenever we need to make a decision, all we have to do is ask ourselves 'What's the worst that could happen?'. Then we work out what we would do in detail if that did happen. Once we know we could handle the worst, there's no reason not to try. Obviously, if we really can't think how we could cope with the worst, we don't take the risk.

One thing you may have noticed, I have repeatedly mentioned research and training. That's because to make money in this world you've got to be good. 'Average' or 'Acceptable' isn't enough. Set your sights high. We're talking about subjects that you're interested in anyway, so it's not gonna feel like hard work to practise or study.

Confidence Is King

Confidence and courage are Siamese twins, joined at the hip. They never go anywhere alone. All of us has a hobby, skill, talent, or idea which we could make money from, but we will never be ready to take risks until we have the confidence to believe in ourselves and our ideas. This is such an important topic that it will be discussed fully in another chapter. For now, just take my word for it; you'll never be rich if you don't believe in yourself.

There's No Such Thing As 'Get Rich Quick'

Ask any rich and successful person about the hours they work, and you'll find they do between one and a half and twice as many as the average. What you'll also find is that they don't mind it, because they're doing something they enjoy, something they're interested in. Earning serious money takes time and hard work. Don't be fooled by those who say they made enormous amounts of money in a short space of time. Ask them what they were doing for the previous five years. Chances are, whether they're aware of it or not, they were learning about their industry, either through their own mistakes, or by working for less money for someone else.

Network Marketing

'Get rich quick' schemes seem to be everywhere nowadays: for example, some of us have been approached by multi-level marketing companies (I won't mention any names). For those who haven't been, let me summarize briefly.

These companies try to get you to join up and buy a sample of their products. You must then persuade other people to do the same. Once you've persuaded a certain number of people to join, you make some money. When the people you persuaded bring others on board, you all make something and live happily ever after.

The reason this is popular is because in theory you can simply spend a few hours a week on it and reap all the benefits. Most, if not all of these businesses are perfectly legitimate. My concern is that they constantly tell you about the thousands of pounds you can earn, or cars you can own, without being totally clear about how long it takes to sign up so many people. They'll all wheel out their star salespeople who are earning thousands every month. What they don't emphasize is that these stars have been in the business for ages, or are doing this full-time.

Occasionally, you'll see those who, by signing up all their

family and friends, made some money, but then when they'd exhausted this supply, things stopped improving. Finally, although you're told you are self-employed, you, and all those you sign up, pay a fixed amount to the company every month. Some may find this an ideal way to make some extra cash . If so, good luck to you. However, as I said before, you never get really rich by working for other people.

Even winning the lottery or at the races isn't a way to get rich quick. You often have to be prepared to bet (or shall we say 'invest'?!) for years before you see any readies. The same applies to the stock market, slot machines and premium bonds. Don't get me wrong, I wish happiness to all those who do manage to win large amounts of money. It's just that this book is for the vast majority of us who don't even win a prize in a school fair raffle.

The Future Is Here

Various estimates throughout the Western world indicate that by the year 2000, at least half of us will be working for ourselves or for small companies. The days of the giant multinationals are numbered. We have three choices: We can be cockroaches, cats, or corpses. Let me explain.

Cockroaches

Although disliked by everyone apart from each other, cockroaches have some qualities worth mentioning. They are naturally adaptive. Regardless of their environment, they adapt to survive all the poisons and chemicals we use to try to kill them. It's been said that they are the only species likely to survive nuclear fall-out. They are not dependent on others for their survival, but rather make a habit of looking at what's around them, and make the most of it. They are constantly assessing their environment, and developing the necessary skills/ powers to master it.

Cats

Much more popular, the cat has sacrificed its independence and much of its instinct to gain favour with others. A once independent and proud animal has become lazy, relying on others to provide what it needs, whilst offering little in return.

It is believed that cats can never be fully tamed. When their instincts lead them to bring home dead mice or birds, they quickly learn the difference between acceptable and unacceptable behaviour, and revert to domesticity to avoid rejection. They can help those around them to relax, but a growing number of substitutes which fulfil this role have made them less desirable. If thrown out or abandoned by those who provide for them, they desperately seek new owners, or become pitiful scavengers, surviving rather than living.

Corpses

These serve no useful purpose whatsoever, and are even more unpopular than cockroaches for the uncomfortable feelings they cause. It is generally considered desirable to remove them from sight at the earliest opportunity, from which time they will only be thought about by their few closest relatives and associates. Corpses are either removed quickly, or left to decay alone slowly. Either way, they are soon unrecognizable as the once great human beings they were. From the moment a person becomes a corpse, they rely on memories to elicit respect or pity.

What's It To Be?

So what do I mean when I say we have to choose between these three? Well, we can choose to look around us, and learn how to survive in a changing world, mixing only with others who share our desire to be independent. This will involve accepting that few people genuinely want us to succeed, but also the comfort of knowing that we control our own destinies.

Second, we can choose to continue to do what most of us are doing already. i.e. sacrificing our dreams and 'keeping our heads down' for the sake of acceptance. There is however, no guarantee that we will always be employed.

Finally, we can choose to live on past glories as we no longer contribute anything worthwhile to our bosses, families, or society. Eventually all of them will get sick of us and not want us around.

It was no coincidence that I chose a cockroach as a symbol of the most desirable character. Just as a lot of rich people are hated, and their faults highlighted more than their strengths, cockroaches always get a bad press. They don't go out of their way to upset anyone, it's just that people see only the negative aspects of their presence.

Exactly How Much More Do You Want?

All of us say we don't have enough money, but we're not specific about how much more we want. Somehow we feel that with a little more money all of our problems would be solved. Judging by the high divorce rates and substance abuse in Hollywood, all I would say is 'It ain't necessarily so'. This chapter is a bit of a misnomer. It's not that we want more money, it's that we want the things money can buy. What's the difference? Let's see:

If as a kid you ever saved up for anything, whether it was a record, a toy, or a present for your mum, you probably had a money box. Whenever relatives gave you money, or you earned some delivering newspapers, you'd count how much you had altogether and work out how much more you needed.

Answer me this, was it coins and notes you kept picturing or the thing you were going to buy? Did you keep looking at money in your mum's purse, or the item in the shop window? For most of us, the thoughts of buying the thing, and the pleasure it would bring, are what spurred us on.

OK, maybe as a kid you weren't much of a saver. How about when you bought your first car/home/outfit or holiday ? Didn't you spend more time imagining how much pleasure you'd get from it than how many coins and notes you'd have to have?

The point is that we can get more motivated about a specific object than we can about a pile of money. What we need to start doing, is setting ourselves specific goals for the things we want. If we want a £10,000 car, and need to save £1,000 deposit, then we break it down into how much we can afford to save each month, and stick to it. We also stop using negative or defeatist language. So whenever anyone asks, we tell them we're going to buy a secondhand BMW in March, not 'If I had the money, I'd like a flashy car'.

I'm not stupid, I realize that often the problem is that on your current income, you can't afford to save anything. Fine, work out how much you feel you need to live on each month, and make sure you include the amount you need to save. Then you know that what you're aiming for is a job which pays that amount each month.

Before we work out the steps you need to take to get this better paid job, let's calculate our desired income. Treat this as a chance to really aim high. Don't just put down the bear minimum you need to survive. Include the cost of nights out, holidays, new clothes and all the other things you deserve. Let me worry about 'being realistic'. I want you to dream!

If you don't know the price of something you want, go and find out. Half the people who go to car showrooms, estate agents, or designer shops don't have the money yet. They just want to have something to aim for. People with money expect the best of everything, including service, so get into the habit now. Sales staff are there to serve you. That's not to say you treat them like dirt, just that you don't have to be apologetic when you ask them questions or want to browse.

One important note – Don't sign anything, join anything, pay anything, or even give them your name. It's their job to find out what you're interested in and to try to make a quick sale. However attractive their sales terms, and however much they tell you that this special offer ends today, don't give in. When we've achieved our goal, and found a way to make more money, then we'll be ready. The last thing I want is for you to increase your problems by trying to get too much too quickly. (End of lecture!)

Grab a calculator and pencil, and hold on to your hats. You're about to plan your future!

PERSONAL SPENDING PLAN

Monthly cost (£)

Rent/Mortgage ....

Bills – gas, lecky, water ....

Food ....

Clothes ....

Transport ....

Children ....

Health ....

Entertainment ....

Beauty ....

Gifts ....

Holidays ....

Loans/debts ....

Savings ....

....

TOTAL ....

Multiply Total by 12 for annual spending: ....

Then multiply by 1.3 for (approx) tax/NI ....

Add £1000, just to be sure

TOTAL SALARY NEEDED: (per yr) ....

I reckon some of you are staring at the page in shock right now. Nine times out of ten, when people do this exercise, they can't believe how much money they need just to be happy. No need to panic. All we need is some thought and planning.

The Right Job With The Right Pay

In the chapter on job satisfaction, we analyze your strengths, skills and interests, so we'll know the sort of work you should be doing. We'll also have your action plan, for training and research, so we'll understand what's got to be done. Now all we need to do is find the right job, at the right salary.

If you don't think your future lies with your current employer (or if you don't have one) it's time to do some serious research. Check newspaper cuttings in the library for articles on the company you want to work for. In the last six months, have they launched a new product? What do you know about it? Have they reported record profits? Which of their products are selling well/badly? Which charities do they donate to? What does it say about the M.D. in Who's Who ? What's the name of the Director of Personnel? (Phone up and ask, remembering to check spelling!)

Only when you've found out as much as you can about the organization can you start to work out how you could be useful to them. Do any of your skills, interests or experiences tie in with anything you've read or heard? If the company's laying off staff, do they need freelancers?

If you talk to executive employment agents, they always tell you that a large number of jobs are never advertized. Personally, I think this is true of both executive and junior jobs. No matter how much an employer might insist that she doesn't need any more staff, if she feels a person could seriously help her or her company she'll create a vacancy. This means that you have to stand out as someone who can do more than the average.

Don't waste your time or money writing a standard letter to companies with your CV. That's what Joe Average does, and most of these letters go straight in the bin. You've got to have a strategy, and work through it with military precision. You need to impress the person who has the authority to give you a chance.

By far the most effective way to sell yourself is face to face. Are there any forthcoming public conferences where any senior people from the company will be guest speakers? Book a place and plan a short introduction (maximum two minutes) you can say when you meet the target person at the conference. Make sure you rehearse, and say something which will stick in their minds. Naturally, you must have a business card of some sort. (Scribbling your number on a napkin just isn't going to impress).

If you can't think of a way to meet someone from the company, you'll have to write the sort of letter that makes them sit up and take notice. Five simple rules apply:

1) use the person's name – it's an insult to start 'Dear sir/madam', and shows you can't even be bothered to find out what sex they are

2) pay a genuine compliment (your research should've given you at least one positive thing about them)

3) avoid using 'I ' as much as possible (you don't want to put them off by being too self-centred, and anyway, it's themselves and their company they're interested in, not you)

4) only ask for a small favour e.g. can they give you some advice/ meet with you, and

5) thank them for their time.

N.B. It is always a good idea to make friends with the person's secretary/P.A. They can help or hinder your attempts, depending on how nice you are to them. It's not hard, just treat them with the same respect you'd show their boss. In fact, there's no reason why you can't write to the P.A. direct and ask for their advice on how to arrange a meeting with their boss. If they do help you, please don't forget to send them a personal thank you note. We all like to feel appreciated.

What about those who already have a job? We'll look at two individuals – Jane Average, the clerical assistant, and Joe Average, the shop assistant, for some ideas:

Jane is bored stiff at work, and earns just enough to cover her rent and bills. She's also got a few debts which she repays monthly. Being honest with herself, she's realized that she'd be much happier working as a probation officer, where she would be meeting and helping a lot of people everyday, and earning a few thousand more. The course she needs to go on costs several thousand pounds and is full-time, but she can't afford to give up her day-time job to do it. What to do?

First she should apply to do voluntary work at weekends for the probation service in her area, to see if she really likes the work. After a few months, she could apply for one of the Home

Office grants available for people wanting to do the course. As a last resort, there are often special career development loans worth investigating which don't have to be repaid until the course finishes. Meanwhile, she must work out how quickly she can pay off her debts, maybe by cutting back on something, taking in a lodger, getting a job as a part-time barmaid, helping her friend with his mobile disco events or doing some typing for people from home.

I'm afraid the fitness fanatics of the '80s were right – no gain without pain! Obviously, she must also apply to get on the course. When she's finished the course, she'll have an advantage over her classmates, because she'll have had years of experience from the voluntary work. This will also show how dedicated she is. If while she was doing her voluntary work, she developed an area of expertise, she's laughing.

If things are really bleak, and no money-making options appear, the only thing for it is to put the other plans on hold, and devise a strategy for getting promotion (and a payrise/ bonus) at the company she's working for. (See job satisfaction chapter.) She should still try to do even a couple of hours of probation voluntary work a week, for three reasons : a) Because she'll stand a better chance of getting a grant, b) To remind herself what she's aiming for, and c) because experienced people can always command a higher salary.

Now, what about our mate Joe? The poor thing's been working for three years in the same shop, packing shelves and serving on the till. On the money he's earning, he could only afford a secondhand car, which keeps breaking down. The one he really wants costs £12,000 new. Joe likes working in a shop, but notices a lot of things he'd do differently, if he were in charge. Simple – let's get him promotion!

To earn the money he needs for his dream car, he would have to be promoted three grades higher. On the other hand, if he became a sales rep, or a buyer, a company car would be thrown in. His task is therefore to talk to those who are already doing these jobs, and to find out what he needs to do to join them. After that, he'll have to plan what he intends to do each week or month to get where he wants to be. (Including getting extra training, going out on the road with a rep, and telling his manager of his ambitions.)

Unemployed Doesn't Mean Unemployable

A special word for those of you who don't have a job: The first thing you must do is become a specialist. If you're unemployed, the government funds a wide range of training courses you can go on, so decide what you want and book a place. (Often they pay you a little bit extra too.) With some basic training under your belt, you select the top 20 companies you'd like to work for, who would be interested in your skills.

If you need some practical experience, you can either offer your services for free, as I did when I started training, or you can ask the unemployment office to approach employers on your behalf, on one of those schemes where the government shares the cost of your wages.

Another alternative is to offer your services to a voluntary organization. You can't afford to have a bad attitude about working for free. Look on it as an investment in your future. As with everything else in this book, you've got to be prepared to give in order to receive.

Self-Employed Specialists

Earlier in this chapter, I mentioned that no one got rich by working for other people, so the long-term goal for the seriously ambitious amongst us has to be self-employment. As there's no such thing as a job for life, and any of us can be made redundant, regardless of our years of service and position, we should start planning now.

If you were handed a redundancy letter tomorrow, what would you do? (No, I mean after you'd shouted and cried.) Would it be worth looking for a similar job, so that someone else could have the chance to do the same to you again? Also, if your company is 'downsizing' (i.e. reducing staff numbers), chances are others in your industry are too.

There is however, a positive side to all this. (They don't call me 'Silver-lining-Myers' for nothing!) More and more companies, in their efforts to save money, have realized that it's cheaper to hire specialists as and when they need them, rather than employ them full-time. Therefore, it's in our own interest to become specialists in something we're interested in, and to offer our services as consultants.

Yes, there are already thousands of consultants in almost every industry, but not that many are brilliant at what they do. Quite a few don't even bother to learn much about what they're doing. Once we've been on training courses, had some work experience, and read everything we can get our hands on about our subject, we will automatically be in the top 10%.

Even if we hate the idea of 'going it alone', we'll have made ourselves more valuable to our employers, and in a better position to get promotions and payrises. We'll also be in a position to do small pieces of work for other companies in our spare time. That way, we'll have a foot in the door if we ever want to work for them full-time. (Check your employment contract. Some don't allow you to have more than one job.)

Let Everyone Know How Good You Are

Knowing our stuff isn't enough. We've got to be able to let the right people know how good we are. This is known as 'self-promotion' in the trade. The suggestions below should spark off ideas of your own, and get you started. (Just make sure you remember me when you make your first million).

1) Go to the library/newsagent and read a copy of every journal or magazine produced for people in your field. Jot down the editors' names and the contact addresses. Then, when you have an original idea about your work, or discover something which may be of interest to others, you write a short article and send it in. (Don't give away any company secrets.)

   If you get a couple of pieces published in a magazine, they may commission you to write more regularly, for a fee. Also, others in the industry will start to regard you as a bit of a bright cookie, so job offers may come your way. At the very least, it might surprise others in your company just how dazzling you are.

2) Volunteer to speak at meetings and conferences. (If you're not a confident speaker, read the confidence chapter, and go on a presentation skills course.) Start small with company events, and move up to industry wide ones. Soon,

you'll be getting paid bookings/respect/promotion/job offers.

3) Come up with a memorable phrase to describe what you're good at: Telling people I do human M.O.T.s is much more interesting than saying that I'm a training consultant. Add to this a distinctive business card and people will get in touch. (If your company won't supply them, get some personal ones printed, and hand them out at every opportunity you get.)

4) Offer to deliver a training course for junior staff, to save your company money. (You'll get your just rewards in time.)

5) Contact training companies, colleges and schools, offering your specialist knowledge for a fee, or on a freelance/part-time basis. (Again, you might have to do some work for free, if they don't know you. If so, try to make them agree to hire you if they're impressed. Then knock 'em dead.)

6) Become famous! Not as difficult as it sounds. I've been on several chat shows and current affairs programmes. All it takes is a phonecall. If you're lucky, they'll be discussing your favourite subject. Even if they aren't, find something interesting to say, so you get the camera on you. Quite a few of my customers saw my 30 seconds of fame on each programme, and were pretty impressed.

7) Find or develop an original angle on what you do. (Marketing people call this a Unique Selling Point.) Whether you're a hairdresser or a builder, a manager or a secretary, you know your job better than most. You probably already do some things a bit differently to others, or to how you were trained, simply because it makes more sense, or saves time. Take the credit you deserve. Write about it, tell people about it, or get someone to do a feature on you in the company newsletter, or industry journal. Show your superiors that you're smarter than the average bear, and they'll start thinking about you as promotion material, not redundancy fodder.

This is no time to be shy. If you don't let it be known that you're brilliant, someone else will end up benefiting from all of the extra bucks you could have been making.

So, making more money involves developing the skills you already have, to become the respected expert you know you can be. Once you're seen as an expert, you will be expected to keep coming up with new ideas, and to keep up to date with what's going on in your industry. That's why it's so important to choose something you enjoy.

Whether you choose to knit baby clothes in the evenings, mend neighbours' cars at weekends, or provide information to holidaymakers on the places you've visited, the message is the same. Be the best at what you do, and you'll get more than extra money. You'll have a sense of achievement, job satisfaction, respect and peace of mind.

I can almost hear the 'but' people singing their dawn chorus: 'But I'm too old to start a business' , 'But I couldn't study and bring up a family at the same time' , 'But my boss would never pay for me to get extra training', 'But I've been unemployed for years', etc. etc.

My answer is simple – IT's NEVER TOO LATE, AND ANYTHING IS POSSIBLE WHEN YOU DECIDE TO REALLY GO FOR IT.

So you're 60 years old. Big deal! Your life expectancy is 70–75 years, so what do you plan to do for the next 10–15? Sit in an armchair and discuss your corns? The idea is to live your life to the full, right up to the last minute. Sprinters don't run 80 yards and give up, looking lost. They give it all they've got till they cross the finishing line. With all your knowledge and experience, I'd say it's your duty to come out here and teach us younger ones some of what you know. If you don't, all that valuable information will be lost forever.

The first step to getting anything we want in life is to *decide* that we're gonna get it. After that, we can come up with ideas on how. Until we promise ourselves that we'll do it, and believe that we're good enough, all we'll have is frustration. Every time we catch ourselves thinking about reasons why we might fail, we must stop, and switch to thinking of reasons why we must succeed. You know as well as I do, that if you want something bad enough, you'll find a way. Well, this is the test: if you really want more money, start jotting down some ideas on how you're gonna get it. If you're not prepared to put in the extra time and effort, quit moaning and just accept things as they are.

All of us are basically decent human beings, who would like to help others in some small way. Perhaps when we start making more money, we can decide to donate a small percentage to a charity each month. My mum says 'What goes around comes around'. Have you noticed how rich people give away millions every year, but never seem to get any poorer? Maybe she's right.

Money is like muck. No good unless it's spread around.

THOMAS BACON (1561–1626)

CHAPTER THREE

I Want More . . . Respect

People get the respect they deserve.

MY BROTHER, TERENCE

What is respect? Lots of people say they want it, or that they give it, without being able to explain what they mean. As a child, many of us were told: 'Respect your elders'. To me, this meant never answering back, never challenging what was said to me, and never telling adults when they were wrong.

Now that I'm a 'grown up', I certainly don't mean this when I say that I respect someone. Respect is another of those words we've misused so much, we've almost ruined it. Just as we can love 10 different people for different reasons, we can respect 10 people for different reasons.

Measuring Up To Our Ideals

My theory is, people who are respected are those who come closest to our ideal image of how someone in their position should be. Thus, a teacher who makes lessons interesting, and encourages his pupils to think will be respected. Why? Because that's close to our ideal image of a teacher. A gang leader will be respected if she is aggressive to outsiders and loyal to friends. That's what's expected of her.

Parents who 'walk their talk' i.e. live up to the standards

they set their kids, will gain respect. It's a popular myth that kids lose respect for us if we discipline them. We only lose their respect when we're not consistent or fair. Police officers and judges will be respected (yes, even by criminals!) if they are seen to be fair, and treat people as equals.

If we look at the people who have already earned our respect, we find it's usually down to more than just how much money they've earned. It's a combination of what they've achieved, their personalities, their speech, and most important, their behaviour. No one respects a hypocrite.

Self-Respect

While we're on the subject, we should touch on self-respect. When we don't respect ourselves, we let people walk all over us.

Maybe we're not living up to our own standards, and that's why we don't think we deserve to be treated well by anyone else. If that's the case, we have two choices: either we change our behaviour until we do live up to the standards we set ourselves, or we rethink our standards and decide if they're realistic. All too often, we expect perfection from ourselves while accepting other people 'warts and all'. Be fair – if you wouldn't expect it from others, don't demand it of yourself.

Disrespect

When people don't live up to our expectations of how they should be in their role, then we 'diss' them. (Just to show how trendy I am, I thought I'd include a little street talk!) 'Diss' is short for Disrespect. Although everyone's experiences will vary, most of us have been in situations where we've felt 'dissed'. Let's look at a few of the more common dissing situations we've all experienced:

1. People don't turn up for arranged meetings, or are always late.

The message is plain – they don't think we're as important as whatever else is going on in their lives, but are too rude and spineless to say so. They also don't think we have the confidence or courage to penalize or punish them. Harsh? Not at all. When someone doesn't turn up, or is late, they realize that we'll be wasting our time waiting for them, but they don't care. The implication is that our time isn't as valuable as theirs (arrogant so and so's) or that we're such doormats we'll always forgive them.

Take it from one who was habitually late for years. Although consciously I never intended to 'diss' anyone, I analyzed my feelings when people were late for me (anger, frustration and indignance), and eventually broke the habit (more or less). The bottom line is, the longer we let them get away with it, the more they'll do it. There are several potential solutions – choose whichever you're most comfortable with:

A) ARRANGE A TREAT.

Let them learn by missing out, whether it's doughnuts with coffee at a meeting, buying a round of drinks, or taking everyone to the seaside for the day. Decide to wait no more than 20 minutes, then get on with it. And don't compromise – latecomers get nothing!

B) ANNOUNCE A PENALTY.

Give a warning when everyone's present that latecomers will be asked to pay for snacks/buy their own drinks/be locked out or have to take the minutes of the meeting. Again, the name of the game is no compromise and no exceptions.

C) EXPLAIN YOUR SIDE.

Take time to explain why it's important for you that people are on time and the consequences of their lateness. It may be that if your date is half an hour late, you become so frustrated that the night is ruined for both of you. Perhaps when your staff are late for a meeting, you miss seeing your children before they go to bed. Maybe others' inconsideration means you miss your evening class or sports practice. If that's the case, explain that these activities are a form of relaxation to you, and missing them will make you difficult to live with, or stressed at work. (The implication is that you're doing these things to be a nicer person to live/ work with, and so it's in their interest to support you.)

2. People don't do what we ask them to.

The first thing that springs to mind is, how are we asking them? Yes, we might be saying 'please', but do we explain why? Do we make it seem like the thing really needs to be done, or that we'll appreciate it if they do it?

Would we do something just because someone asked us to? Aren't we more likely to get things done when we can see it's really important or will be appreciated? Subconsciously, we all work on the principle that if a thing isn't worth doing, it isn't worth doing well! If this form of 'dissing' is our problem, it's not so much that people don't respect us. We're not treating them with respect.

We must take into account the fact that everyone (including kids) considers their time to be valuable. They want to be appreciated for what they do, even if they're paid to do it. By making the effort to explain why something needs to be done, and why it will be appreciated, we're likely to find that they do even more than we asked them to.

I'll give you a couple of examples to prove the point. If our manager asked us to read through last year's customer files, we either wouldn't get round to it, or we'd do it in a half-hearted and bored way. If, however, we were told that somewhere in the files was a mistake which cost the company millions, and would result in job losses unless we found it, we'd probably get it done in a couple of days. Following on from that, if finding the mistake would save our boss her job, she would certainly appreciate our efforts.

Telling the kids to tidy their rooms might not get results. On the other hand, explaining that tidying their rooms while we clean the kitchen would mean that we have the time (and energy) to take them out for a treat, might make a difference.

Hopefully, you've noticed something else about getting people to do what you ask them to: If you can find a direct benefit for them, you're on to a winner.

3. People use our things without asking first.

We've all had this happen, whether it's brothers, sisters, partners or friends. The items in question can vary from our clothes, to our razors, our cars or our money. The underlying message here is that we are less important than them, so we don't deserve the same treatment they would expect. Most of us must be guilty of having done this at some time or other, so analyzing our own behaviour can help us to understand what's going on.

When I was about 13, I not only borrowed my sister's clothes, but also my brother's. (I was a big ska fan, and he had heaps of Fred Perry jumpers and T-shirts, which I couldn't afford.) I feel obliged to include my greatest sin, as I'm in a confessional mood – I once cut up and altered a pair of his 'tonic' trousers to wear to a disco, while he was out! (Maybe it wouldn't have been so bad if we'd had a sewing machine, but we didn't, so I altered them by hand.) Although I was brought up to know better, somehow, I let my immediate desires (to look cool and impress my friends) become more important than my respect for another's property. I knew my brother would be upset, but I took advantage of how close we were, and the fact that he would always forgive me.

This behaviour may sound extreme, but how different is it from the woman who blunts her man's razor by using it to shave her legs? Or the man who takes a tenner out of his part-ner's purse to go for a drink with his mates?

Because all of our parents bring us up to know right from wrong, we are fully aware of what we're doing. What we're basically saying, however is 'You love me, so I know you'll for-give me. After all, this isn't a big enough sin to cause the breakdown of our relationship.' We then have the cheek to get angry when the other person gets upset, and tell them to either stop nagging, or that it's no big deal. (In my brother's case, I figured a simple apology after the event would be enough. It wasn't, but he did forgive me eventually.)

One thing that's struck me is that we don't tend to do this with people we don't know very well, or people who we're not close to. The bottom line is that we know in our hearts that our behaviour isn't a million miles away from theft, and most of us would be horrified to be accused of stealing. Those close to us, however, although they may shout a bit, never call us harsh names like 'thieves'. Of course, if we ever did what we say we intend to do i.e. replace what we'd used, then it would simply be 'borrowing'. But how often do we get round to it?

We decide subconsciously that the ideal for those who love us is that they should always forgive us. Teenagers who take their parents' car without permission are definitely working on this logic. Trouble is, being forgiven doesn't make us respect people more. It just encourages us to go further and see how much else we can get away with. My theory is that humans are more like other animals than we care to admit, and so we look for weaknesses to exploit, just as other animals do.

STEALING FROM OUR LOVED ONES

So what's the solution? Well, if we're the guilty ones, we've got to start being honest with ourselves and admit that what we are actually doing is stealing from those we care most about. Think about it – stealing is simply taking something which doesn't belong to us, without asking permission from the owner. To clear our consciences, we must ask before we take something, and accept that the other person does have the right to say 'no'. Putting ourselves in their shoes should help. How would we feel if every time we went to use something, it had disappeared or was broken?

If it's someone else who's guilty of treating our possessions with scorn, drastic action is called for. By now, we've probably realized that nagging/moaning/ shouting is not going to achieve anything other than raise our blood pressure. So we stay calm, and make a list of five of their possessions they use regularly. (Don't choose his best golf clubs or her £500 tennis racket. We want to teach a lesson, not end the relationship!) The sort of things I mean are cds, ties, jackets, special toiletries, computer disks (always save on a back up first), 10-year-old whisky, videos of their favourite sporting moments (again, save on a spare first), or their (cheap) push-bike.

Each time they disrespect you by stealing your property, one of theirs 'disappears'. The reason for choosing things they use regularly, is that they'll notice what's happening, and learn their lesson quicker. The last thing you want is for this to drag on forever. When they ask what's happened to their stuff, you put on the same innocent voice they use with you, and make out they're being unreasonable to get upset. It is important to stay calm. We want them to realize that we are reflecting their behaviour. If they think this is some vindictive campaign, all hell will break loose, and I personally don't want to be on the receiving end of poison pen letters from your angry partners and kids.

One final word of warning: don't withhold your love/sex as a 'punishment'. Re-read the chapter on love until it sinks in that love is not something you give conditionally. You'd be horrified if your mother said she didn't love you any more, because you borrowed her make-up or car, wouldn't you? Well, if you're mature enough to understand that disliking someone's behaviour is different from disliking them, don't jeopardize what you have.

4. We don't get the support we expect in public.
Whatever's going on in our personal or professional relationships, we never want the outside world to see anything other

than a united front. Thus, we get really angry when our boss-es/ staff/ partners/parents disagree with us in public, or worse, show up our weaknesses in public. And boy, do we take a long time to forgive them?! Why do they do it? Two main reasons – because they're not aware of the effect their speech or actions are having on us, or second, to settle the score on some previous grievance.

In the love chapter, I recommended that we don't go to sleep on an argument. Well, perhaps we ought to extend this and say, don't go to a meeting with an unresolved argument, and certainly don't go out socializing with anger in your heart. Apart from being rude to those around you by making them feel uncomfortable while you argue, you will also give a very negative impression of yourself, which will be remembered long after the argument is forgotten. Don't wait for the other person to sort things out. That just wastes time. You must take the initiative.

HIDDEN COSTS OF AIRING GRIEVANCES

Just in case any of you are still in any doubt, let me emphasize how unprofessional it is to air grievances publicly: Some of you may have expected promotion in the past, and felt cheat-ed when it never arrived. Believe it or not, those with the power to decide on promotions might still remember how negative you were to your boss in a meeting two years ago. Their logic will be 'If that's how they treat their managers, I don't want them working for me.' Of course, this will never be said, and you could go on wondering why you're constantly overlooked. Why not be the sort of person everyone wants to work for them? If you're a boss, be the sort that everyone wants to work for. Then you'll have the best in the company trying to move into your department.

I'm painfully aware that I may have lost some of you, who don't really understand what I mean by 'support'. As we've come this far together, I'd hate to lose you now. So the bright sparks among you, who already understand, please bear with us a moment.

Support can be anything from being seen to enthusiastically agree with someone (a grudging 'yes' isn't good enough), to arming yourself with all the facts and figures relevant to the meeting, so that you can come to the rescue if anyone tries to catch your boss out.

Socially, it can be praising your partner's achievements, or defending their honour (yes, even against your best friend). Get the idea? Good. Let's move on.

ARE WE BEING UNREASONABLE?

If you take my advice and resolve arguments beforehand, then we can assume that any lack of support is a result of the other person not understanding what you expect from them. Calmly explaining why you were disappointed in their behaviour can be highly effective. It also means you have to think about whether your reasons for being upset are legitimate.

I once got upset when, after a man had spilt his drink over me in a club, my partner simply asked him to apologize. I wanted him to punch the guy in the face (I guess it was the Neanderthal in me coming through!) My partner, who was never a violent person, didn't know what to say to me. Luckily, I took a couple of minutes to think, and quickly realized that I was being ridiculous, as the guy *had* apologized.

5. People take us for granted/ignore our feelings.

This includes forms of 'dissing' already discussed, and more. It can occur in the workplace or in personal relationships. Closely linked with using our possessions without permission, people who 'diss' us in this way are treating us badly because they know we'll forgive them. Letting people treat us like dirt is a sign that we don't love ourselves enough. Study every syllable of the love chapter, and put a stop to this.

6. Our rights are violated.

The American Declaration written in 1776, stated that:

> *We hold these truths to be self-evident, that all men are created equal, that they are endowed by their Creator with certain unalienable rights, that among these are life, liberty, and the pursuit of happiness.*

For the moment, we'll forgive them for ignoring half of the population (i.e. women), and concentrate on the philosophy. Those who do not recognize our rights to the above are often those with the power to treat us badly, who know that we will have a hard time fighting them. The weakest in our society are often not in a position to fight alone.

Many who can't personally afford to fight huge legal battles against large corporations, the government, or the police, start fundraising campaigns. All this involves is letting the media know what we're doing, and asking everyone we know to help us. Often, a slightly wealthier or more powerful individual will take up our cause. If we know of, or hear of, someone who has had their rights violated, my gut feel is that it's our duty to support them in any way we can, to stop it happening again in the future.

Whether we've been unfairly sacked because of our colour, refused employment because of our sex, or discriminated against in law, we must find supporters and fight. Of course, the surest way to fight the violation of rights is to become part of the system which holds the power and influence. Become a local councillor/Member of Parliament/lawyer police officer/journalist or business owner. We must find out what we need, in terms of qualifications and experience, and get started. It's never too late. We're either part of the solution, or part of the problem.

We Can't Demand Respect

Respect is something which we all deserve and desire. It is not something that we can demand or win by force. (For the parents amongst us, I know I'm preaching to the converted.) We've all tried to cut corners by demanding the respect we want, before we've shown that we deserve it. And we've all learnt, or are learning, that there are no short cuts. Our most consistent behaviour is what we are judged on. One respectable deed means nothing amongst a month of bad treatment.

Realistically, we will not be respected by everyone for everything we do. Therefore choices have to be made.

Take a moment to answer the following:

1) In what areas of my life am I most disrespected?

A) ....

B) ....

C) ....

2) In each of these areas, what would be ideal behaviour for someone in my position?

A) ....

B) ....

C) ....

3) What can I do to earn the respect I want?

....

....

....

4) Who can I ask for an honest opinion on why I'm not respected? (If you can't think of anyone, ask those who are 'dissing' you)

....

....

....

5) Based on what I've read, is there anyone who I'm 'dissing'?

....

....

....

6) What am I going to do about it?

....

....

....

Good luck, and enjoy the greater understanding which is sure to come.

The Revenge Seekers

Sometimes, we have to deal with people who appear to be totally unreasonable. They don't respect our views, our rights or our feelings. These are what I call revenge seekers. Because no one ever showed them any respect, they neither want to or are able to show any to others. Because other people made them feel worthless, they try to make us feel equally bad.

When these people are put in a position of power, be that in an organization, a police force, a school or a family, they are dangerous. Their self-esteem is so low that the only way they can feel important is by abusing their power and making others feel inferior.

I've worked for people like this in two organizations. When I tried to discuss the problem, they saw it as a sign of weakness. When I tried to fight back, they pulled rank. When I tried to ignore them, they became worse. There were a lot of wet pillow nights, I can tell you.

As always, hindsight is a wonderful thing, so it wasn't until after I'd left both organizations that I learnt how to deal effectively with these managers from hell.

Ensuring Respect At work

The most important thing is to remain professional. Screaming, shouting, physical violence, public tears, or snide comments are out. These will simply lose you respect and support from others in the team or organization. Instead, for the next month, you must make a note of dates and times when you were abused or disrespected. (I know it's hard, but be patient. It'll be worth it in the end.) At the end of that month, request a private meeting with the person concerned. Above all else, you must be calm.

In your meeting, you tell them that you believe you are being unfairly and improperly treated, and let them know the occasions in the last month when this has occurred. Explain that you want to sort this out with them quickly, but you will continue to monitor the situation, and if their treatment of you doesn't improve, you will take the matter to personnel/senior management.

Listen to anything they have to say, and make notes of it. Finally, ask them if there are any specific problems they have with you or your work. (Again, note down what they say.) This will frighten some of them to buck up. Others will get angry or worse.

Whatever their response, when you have finished, you return to your work, and make no further reference to what was said. For the next month, you continue as before, making sure that your work is exceptional, and that you are never late, even if they are. (They might start trying to find reasons to get rid of you.)

If things haven't improved after another month, you arrange a meeting with personnel/senior management, and explain that your attempts to rectify the situation have failed. Make it clear that you will go to an industrial tribunal if this isn't dealt with. (Be sure not to take your anger and frustration out on these people, as they are probably not aware of what you've been suffering.) Finally, you monitor things for one more month, and if need be, take legal advice. If your notes of incidences are requested by anyone, always keep a copy.

It's horrible to have to go through all this, and believe me, I wouldn't recommend it if I thought there was any other way. But remember, at the end of the day, we all have a right to be able to get on with our jobs without having to put up with abuse.

Family Domination

I'm on less solid ground here, as my family are brilliant. That's not to say that as the youngest, my brothers and sisters never pulled rank, or my parents never told us what to do, just that as with most people, I knew they all had my best interests at heart. (My family must be smiling reading this. They always said I'd understand better when I grew up!)

Things are much more difficult when a relative is disrespecting us, simply because we are only protected by law from the most serious forms of dissing. Plus, we're brought up to keep quiet, and not wash our dirty laundry in public. Whether it's our kids, our parents, or our siblings who are treating us like dirt, we are expected to see it as the price we have to pay for being a family member.

One possible solution might be to involve another person – a grandparent, aunt, priest, neighbour or cousin. Basically, if there is anyone who the hurtful person is close to who would be willing to talk to them, it's worth asking them to have a word on your behalf.

If none of the suggestions already mentioned work within our homes, we must decide a course of action which is based on our rights to be treated well. Fewer visits, or leaving home, are the painful last resort solutions. I can't tell what is right for every situation, but there is a basic principle I believe in, which was beautifully summed up by something a friend of mine, Rasheda, once said:

'No one has the right to rain on your dreams, and you have no business letting them.'

The most important advice I can give is to remind you of the importance of trying to talk things through calmly. Often our relatives aren't aware of just how much their speech and behaviour is affecting us. And even if they are, they may stop when they realize that we are seriously considering moving out or stopping visits.

Sex and Respect

A couple of years ago, I came home so angry after a shopping trip that I wrote a short article which I originally intended to send to editors of male magazines and all of the nationals. Even though I never got round to finishing it, or sending it, I felt better after taking out my rage on paper. The article was called:

I AM SOMEBODY'S DAUGHTER

I am somebody's daughter. I am somebody's sister. One day, I will be somebody's mother. But in the street, I am nothing. When men look at me, they do not see their own daughters, who they would protect with their lives, or their nurturing mothers, who they would never raise their voices to.

I am a woman alone in the street, and therefore, it is assumed, I must be looking for a man. When their wives and mothers leave the house, is it because they want sex, or because they have to go to work, collect kids from school, visit relatives, or do the shopping?

Sometimes, I walk on the street after dark. I don't have a

car, but I do have a life. I walk quickly from the station to my house, avoiding poorly lit streets and alleyways. I don't think I'm better than anybody else, but my life and my body are special to me. Is it so hard to understand that when a man tries to talk to me in the street, I feel scared?

Reason tells me that he may be a perfectly kind and friendly person. My survival instinct says not to stop and chat, in case he isn't. If I am then shouted and sworn at, I feel guilty, because I was not brought up to be rude and ignore people.

If I say hello, it is not assumed that I am a polite person, but that I am considering a sexual relationship. Many men are now a lot more sophisticated than the old building site lech, and street corner perv. They wouldn't dream of shouting out to a woman in the street. They would much rather request that a woman 'works late', or just comes for a drink to unwind after work. In these situations, refusal seems rude and unnecessary. The emphasis, just like with the street corner pervs, is on an innocent suggestion.

If a man buys a male colleague a few drinks, does he expect to drive him home or to have at least a good night kiss? When two men work late, does one lean across the other and 'accidentally' brush against his body? I think not. . . .

It's argued that in the '90s it's hard for anyone to know what is acceptable behaviour. After all, we can't stop finding people attractive. This is a cop out. A person who objects to sexual harassment from strangers or colleagues is considered frigid or anti something. Yes, we're anti-dissing.

To explain my position to male friends, I often suggest that before they approach a woman they are attracted to, they imagine how they would want a man to speak to their daughter, and then follow that example. Not to be sexist, I must add that the same principle applies to women chatting up men, and homosexuals speaking to same sex individuals: If you wouldn't like someone to say it to your mother/father/son or daughter, don't say it.

From the victims' point of view, it's important to never let the harassers think their behaviour or speech is acceptable. With strangers in the street, simply ignoring them might be best. In slightly safer situations, reminding the person that you're somebody's daughter/child/parent too should shut them up long enough for you to explain. (If you think it's worth it.)

The workplace can be difficult, because everything is often done so innocently, you spend half the time wondering if it was just your imagination. Nine times out of 10 it wasn't – your colleague is a lech! Try humour with a sting in the tail: 'The next time you accidentally brush against my chest, my knee will accidentally brush against your groin.'

They'll probably act hurt, shocked or upset, but they'll get the message. If you experience anything more serious, follow the same procedure as that for ensuring respect in the workplace.

Another type of subtle harasser is the person who preys on the self-employed. They give the impression that they can potentially give us heaps of work, but 'the only time I'm free to meet is evenings and weekends'. Don't fall into this trap, however desperate for work you are. Business people meet between 8am and 6pm.

Ask yourself whether they would expect a manager of a large corporation to meet them in a winebar after hours. If the answer is no, suggest day-time meetings. You can legitimately explain that due to personal commitments, you have to conduct all business before 6 o'clock. Any genuine person will respect this. If you really aren't sure about their intentions, take a colleague or associate along, and see how annoyed they are by this. The more annoyed, the more dishonourable their intentions.

Racism and Respect

This topic deserves separate attention, because it is the exception to the rule about why we respect or diss people. In most cases, respect is shown to those who live up to our personal expectations. Racists start off with low, negative expectations about others and don't respect them whether they live up to them or not.

As Martin Luther King said, 'Ignorance is the root of all racism.' When we don't understand people or their way of life, we try to make them more like us. If they conform, they become part of the 'some' who are all right. If they don't, we're suspicious of them and judge their whole nation on the behaviour of one or two individuals.

It's strange how, even when we see lots of examples which show us how wrong we are, we stubbornly refuse to change our opinions. Yet we'd be horrified if the British were described as drug dealers based on the behaviour of a few stupid individuals caught in South East Asia. How about if the world said we were all alcoholics because so many of us go to pubs regularly?

Disrespecting someone because we don't understand their culture can take many forms. It may be that we assume they are less intelligent, and so talk down to them, or that we laugh at their accents while enjoying their food. It could be that we don't trust them, because we've heard about 'one of them' being dishonest. (When I first tried to open a bank account in north London, I was told I would have to be interviewed first, even though I had a substantial amount to deposit. When I asked if this was standard procedure, I was told that it wasn't, 'but we've had a lot of problems with fraud amongst Nigerians lately'.)

This was frightening in as much as the bank had decided that any black person from any part of the world (Bristol in my case), was likely to be a crook. Well, over the years, I've read hundreds of stories about white middle-class men embezzling company profits or being imprisoned for fraud – does this mean no one should employ white men any more?

If you're the one being dissed, it's worth remembering that it's the other person's ignorance that's causing it. Yes, I know it makes you angry, but we all know that getting angry just reinforces all the worst stereotypes. In the past, I've found that taking the time to get to know people, finding similarities between our cultures, and explaining differences can be valuable. Trying to understand and be understood doesn't mean that either person has to apologize for the way they live, or try to be more like the majority.

Disability and Respect

I have a confession to make: this section has been added after the first draft was complete. Yep, 'right on' as I like to think I am, I still managed to forget the six million disabled people in Britain, and numerous millions around the world. What can I say, except that I'm genuinely sorry, and am now trying to make amends?

Full credit for this section being written must go to LBC Radio – a London independent station. While I was redecorating my flat, I heard an interview they conducted with two guys who had cerebral palsy, but weren't letting it stop them becoming actors. As they discussed all the problems they faced with able bodied people and their attitudes, the penny dropped. I scribbled some notes, and then typed this up later.

We, the able bodied, can be unbelievably stupid when we meet or see a disabled person, especially one who has a visible disability. Our first assumption is that if their bodies aren't quite 'right', then their brains can't be either. Don't get uncomfortable, I'm not pointing the finger, but we've all done it haven't we?

If there's someone pushing their wheelchair, we talk to them, in much the same way that we talk to the parent not the child in the buggy. We never once stop to think how rude it is to ignore someone, or worse, to talk about them while they're there.

My father lost the use of his legs years before the multiple sclerosis finally killed him, but no one ever dissed him. I wonder if we work on the 'some of them are all right' principle that racists use: If we know them personally, we treat them as equals, if we don't, we assume the worst? For years I objected to the way organizations lumped together 'ethnic minorities' and the disabled. I'm still not sure I like it, but I can see how we share common experiences.

So what can we do to improve things? For a start, we can assume the best. It's not as silly as it sounds. If we assume that a person can understand us perfectly well, the way we do with everyone else we meet, then they can always ask us to either explain ourselves, speak more slowly, or face them so that they can read our lips. That way no one is insulted, or made to feel inferior.

By now we all agree that respect involves treating people as equals, 'doing as we would be done by'. On this principle, a quiet 'do you need any help?', is far more respectful than just grabbing someone's arm and dragging them on to the train, or across the road, when we see a white stick.

Often, we feel that we just don't have the time to talk to someone who may take longer than us to get a sentence out, or to socialize with someone who might not be able to get into the places we go to. Perhaps if we could stop for a minute and swap roles, we would see what nasty individuals we are.

With the number of illnesses and disabilities which can occur unexpectedly in adult life, we must all consider how we would cope if everyone treated us the way we treat other disabled people. It's hard to ignore a white stick, wheelchair, dribbling, or missing limbs, and no one expects us to. All we need, is for everyone to remind themselves that *the other person is different not inferior.* There's nothing wrong with being honest – why not say: 'Hey, I've never had a chance to talk to a person with your disability before, so please tell me if I say or do anything to insult you.' If said genuinely, you will be respected for being honest, as well as for taking the time to try to overcome your prejudices. You might also make a valuable friend.

We're As Similar As We Are Different

I was amazed when I found out how similar my West Indian upbringing was to that of my Irish friends. We all had to go to church when we were younger, we all had wakes when someone died, almost all of us had at least one relative who had emigrated to make a better life for themselves, the bookmaker's was regarded as a social club for working men, not a gambling den, we all felt a bit offended when a visitor refused food and drink from us in our homes, it was our mothers who managed the household budget, and amongst all of us saying what was on your mind was not just acceptable, but expected.

These things might seem insignificant, but they made a huge difference. For example, if I visited a friend, and she said her man was 'down the bookies', I didn't think less of him, or pity her, thinking that he was about to lose their mortgage money. I just took it in my stride, and carried on.

By the same token, the Spanish people I've met think my way of speaking to be perfectly normal (I use my hands a lot, and have a loud voice). In Britain, I was shocked to discover that because of this people at work thought I was 'aggressive'.

When we condemn people for not being more like us, we are basically saying that we think our ways are better. Common sense should tell us that every culture has some positive aspects which are worthy of respect, just as the British one does.

Any fool can point out differences, but once we really accept that all of us have some things in common, we can start to relax and accept, not blame and reject. Although it seems unfair, it is often up to us the victims to try to bridge the gap. At first, this is the last thing we feel like doing, but in the long run, it can make for much better relationships, based on mutual respect.

Youth Crime

I feel I can't leave this topic without looking at wider issues. So far, we've concentrated on the reasons for, and solutions to individual dissing. Many of us, however, are concerned with the increasing level of youth crime in our society.

My theory is that there are two main reasons for what's happening. First, when people of any age don't feel part of the gang (whether the gang is society, a family, or a work team) they see no reason to respect others who are.

Be honest, when kids refused to let you join in their games in the playground, you didn't exactly think nice things about them. Just like in meetings, when no one includes us, we give them the silent treatment and harbour resentment. If this exclusion takes place before we're mature enough to think carefully about the consequences of our actions, anti-social behaviour will result.

Second, going back to what was said before, we take advantage when we know we'll be forgiven. Young people know that society will forgive them, so they see no reason to stop. When young people display anti-social behaviour, maybe we should simply do the same to them i.e. if they go 'joy riding', we simply 'borrow' their favourite clothes/records/bike, accidently damage them, and then innocently tell them we just did it 'for a laugh', or 'didn't mean to'.

Hopefully, something like this will help to teach a lesson to the less serious offenders at least. To make them feel part of the gang we call society, maybe we need to give them some responsibility and worthwhile work to do. In fact, it's possible that all they really want is for adults to show them respect, and give them the same opportunities to earn respect that we all need and desire. We all have our own definitions of respect, but the message is the same for the dissed and the dissing: 'Take time to understand and to be understood'.

We owe respect to the living. To the dead, we owe only truth.'

VOLTAIRE (1694–1778)

I Want More . . . Job Satisfaction

Someone is a success if they get up in the morning, and go to bed at night, and inbetween, they do what they want to do.

BOB DYLAN

When I ask most people if they enjoy their jobs, they look at me like I'm some sort of mad woman, or stupid idealist. Typical responses include:

'Well it pays the bills.'
'I suppose I should consider myself lucky to have a job.'
'Be serious! Work is a four-letter word.'

It's obvious that the most common view of work is as a means to an end. We work so that we can have the money to do something we enjoy in our spare time. But when you think that on average we spend more than half of our waking hours at work, that's a large part of our lives we're wasting being frustrated and depressed.

This Ain't Like School

When I got my first job after I graduated, the most important things to me were getting a good salary, and to work for a company with a good reputation. It probably took me no more than a couple of months to realize that I'd chosen badly.

As a *very* small cog in a huge wheel, I got the impression that I was expected to simply turn up, keep my head down and adopt a white, middle-class, male attitude to everything. Unfortunately, though I tried really hard to suppress it, my black working-class (and God forbid, socialist) attitudes kept coming through. Qualities which had served me well all through school, college and university were considered inappropriate in an old, traditional organization.

Why Don't They Warn Us?

I've been arguing for years that schools should concentrate on teaching kids life skills, to prepare them for the real world: throughout my education, I was led to believe that we lived in a meritocratic society, where hard work and honesty were everything.

I genuinely believed that the best person was always the one who was rewarded/ promoted, and that people would appreciate my honesty. No one mentioned petty politics, the importance of who you know, or even the fact that in business, people don't want you to 'tell it like it is'. Boy, did I learn the hard way!

Without painting a totally negative picture, I must be honest and say that there are still some organizations where incompetents and friends of senior managers are promoted faster than those who contribute most.

When Plain English Isn't So Plain

So, not being part of the right gang/not 'fitting in' can be a major reason for many people not feeling satisfied at work. The first thing to recognize is that no amount of moaning about how unfair life is will achieve anything. From my own experience, I can tell you that trying to change your personality doesn't work either: if you're anything like me, you become so frustrated, and lose so much confidence in yourself, that you cry yourself to sleep, and get depressed.

For 19 years of my life, I lived in a city (Bristol), and grew up in a culture (West Indian), where everyone says what's on their minds. At work, this was considered 'aggressive'.

Not having our views and opinions listened to, or not being taken seriously, because we don't phrase things 'correctly', can be frustrating. We must find nice ways of telling people that they don't know what they're talking about, or that they are about to make a major mistake. Below are a few suggestions for you to try :

1. Someone's talking rubbish.
'I'm sorry, I'm having trouble understanding this. Could you explain why you think. . . '

(Follow their next answer with 'Oh, Am I wrong in thinking. . . ' and then tell them the sensible opinion.)

2. Someone who knows little about your job tries to tell you how to do it.

'Can I quickly explain how I do things at the moment, and then you can let me know what you think. . . ' or

'Customers/clients tell me. . . '

3. You have a good idea but no one takes any notice/others think you're a smartass.

'When you've got a minute, can I ask your opinion about something. . . ?' or

'I need your advice: I've got an idea, which I think might be a good one, but I don't know how to present it well. Can I start off by telling you what it is, and then, if you think it's good, maybe you can help me?'

4. You're given all the jobs no one else wants/you're excluded from decision-making.

First decide what you'd like to be involved in. Then find out as much as you can about it. Finally, say to your manager:

'If I make sure all of my work gets done, do you think I could sit in on the next meeting on . . . ? It's just that I'd really like to learn more about the company' or

'I can see how busy you are, so I've taught myself about. . . I'd be happy to help with the more straightforward jobs.'

Stroking

I'm sure you get the idea. Basically, you have to start off by 'stroking' people first, even when you don't like them. In fact, *especially* when you don't like them! If others see you as a threat, so they never include you in important matters, or they have bigoted views on your 'place' in the organisation, the only way to win them over is to show them they're wrong *in the nicest way possible.*

Everyone has to play the game to a certain extent. We have to dress appropriately, and learn to phrase things in acceptable ways. The first was easy for me – ask any of my friends how much I love clothes! The second was a total nightmare.

Dress For Success

I remember being on a Women Into Business course years ago, where the trainer gave a worrying explanation of why many women fail to reach the dizzy heights they're capable of. She used the banking industry as an example. Some survey had shown that when male and female members of staff, of equal ability and intelligence, were applying for promotion, the male usually got the job. Why? Not because all bank managers are sexist dogs, but because the males understood one very fundamental aspect of business – Conservatism Is King. (Ha, your secret's out the bag now!)

Regardless of what they wore in their private lives, at work, the men could always be seen in a suit and tie. (Even those horrible shiny ones with white flecks.) Females, on the other hand, wore the latest fashions, pretty, flowery dresses, jumpers, mini-skirts etc. I must admit, I didn't believe it, but in the last few years, I've made a point of comparing bank cashiers' clothes, and it's true!

Obviously, we are all entitled to wear what we like, but if we want promotion, we've got to look and act like our managers. They won't promote someone who they think gives the wrong image of their company. Think about it – a bank wants the public to see its staff as objective, confident, professionals, not girlies who look like they need protecting, or are about to do the housework. And definitely not sex kittens who'll only agree a loan if you're good looking.

If the company doesn't provide a uniform, invest in a navy suit or two, that is, unless your managers are all wearing hot pants, jumpers and frilly dresses. Outside of the music and fashion industries, (and perhaps the media), it is inappropriate and expensive to be a fashion victim. Save the hip gear for evenings and weekends, and go for the promotion you deserve.

I was once told that we should 'Dress for where we are going, not where we are.' Wise words indeed.

Have You Got A Bad Attitude?

Right, so we know how to phrase things, and what to wear, what else is there? Lots. Take attitude. Isn't it easy to be the ideal worker when the sun is shining, your in-tray's nearly empty, all of your customers think you're wonderful and you're sporting a new hairstyle or outfit? For most of us, however, this is *not* a typical day.

What do we do when we wake up late to the sound of rain, only realize that we have a button missing when a senior manager points it out, haven't seen the bottom of our in-trays since England won the World Cup (before man walked on the moon), and every customer is threatening to return goods or tear up their contracts? We get fed up/depressed/ irritable/angry/frustrated (delete as appropriate). Then we practise the loser's pastime, until we reach Olympic standard.

What's the loser's pastime? Blaming. You know the sort of phrases:

> *'If Distribution did their jobs properly, I wouldn't get all this flack from my customers.' or:*

> *'I can't help it if the report's not finished. Typing said they'd have it ready on time.'*

or even :

> *'I'm just a bit fed up today. I mean, the rain's so depressing.'*

Choosing Your Moods

Let's get one thing straight now. Blaming people or things for our bad performance or mood will simply show everyone what immature, unreliable, unprofessional, people we are. Doesn't exactly put us on the road to promotion and fulfilment does it?

There's a very simple technique which surprisingly few people seem to be aware of: Acting As If. (Also, check out the confidence chapter). If you're fed up because you hate the rain, act as if it were a bright sunny day – smile, sing in the shower, choose something bright and cheerful to wear, and take the time to groom yourself well. 'Oh yes,' you cry, 'but as soon as I get to work, something happens to bring me down to earth with a bump.'

Don't be so pathetic! No one can make you feel anything; love, hate, happy, sad, worthless or special. You choose your reactions to people and situations, and your emotional responses. Oh ye of little faith! Must I always give an example to convince you? OK. After all, that's what you've paid for.

If our boss tells us at 5.30 that she wants us to re-do a piece of work because it's sub-standard, we usually choose to feel annoyed and victimized, thinking about how our plans for the evening are ruined. A month later, we're still seething, and telling anyone who'll listen how much she hates us. Alternatively, we could decide to find out exactly what she's not happy with, and before we get started, make an appointment to see her the next day, and phone anyone we've made plans with, to say we'll be late. In this case, we'll be more motivated to get the job done, knowing our friends are waiting for us. The next day, we could start off by apologizing to our boss for any inconvenience caused. Then we could ask if she'd mind if we spent a bit more time in the future going over work she's requested, to make sure we understand exactly what she expects. This way, we can be confident that the same thing won't happen again, and that our boss will respect our professional, mature attitude. We also won't be getting ourselves stressed, or raise our blood pressure, by harbouring a grudge. Now do you believe me?

Handy Hint

When you're in a fairly good mood, and have time on your hands, compile a few (at least two) tapes of all your favourite songs – ones which you associate with happy memories, or which you always sing along to. Then, while you're getting ready for work, or driving to work, play one of them. Guaranteed you'll arrive in a good mood.

This chapter is about job satisfaction, yet so far we've looked at speech, dress sense and attitude. Why? Because I think that there are a lot of people out there who are not getting the chance to do interesting, challenging work, because they don't realize that they are being judged on these things.

Of course, there are other reasons why some of us are not satisfied in our work, but before we move on to them, I want to have a quick word with the unemployed, the students, and all those about to start a new job. (The rest of you might learn a thing or two for future reference as well.)

Start As You Mean To Go On

When we first get a job (especially nowadays), we feel brilliant, and ready to knock 'em dead. Then we find that for the first three weeks in the company, no one seems to know what we should be doing – least of all us. Naturally, we don't want to confront our managers, but we must do two things :

1) We must keep busy, otherwise colleagues will resent us, and

2) We must gain credibility as quickly as possible, otherwise we'll never be given a chance to work on projects which show off our talents.

One way to avoid this nightmare scenario, where you're all fired up with nothing to do, is to take the initiative from the start. As soon as you've accepted the job offer, you make it your business to find out names of colleagues you'll be working with (especially PAs and secretaries). Then you phone/write and suggest that you meet for lunch – you can lie and say you'll be in the area anyway, so you don't seem like a creep.

At lunch, you let them do most of the talking. The aim is to find out not only what they do, but also, what people think of your new boss, why the last person left, what their main tasks were, what staff morale is like etc. etc . Armed with this valuable market research, which you'll never be told about honestly in an interview, you can then prepare. (Hopefully, you'll still have a couple of weeks before you're due to start work.)

Preparing To Impress

What do I mean by 'prepare?'. If you're going to work in an industry you know little about, or will be using equipment you know little about, book yourself on a short, introductory course. Failing that, buy a couple of books and trade journals, so that by the time you start work, you have at least a basic understanding of what everyone else is talking about.

This process will help you to pinpoint those aspects of the industry or job you find most interesting. The people who are overlooked when opportunities arise are often those who don't seem to have any special areas of expertise or interest, and seem content to just turn up every day. Thus, even if an ideal opportunity does arise, no one is aware that these people would be keen to try it.

Your next task is to find out what makes your immediate manager tick, so phone to arrange a lunch with her/him. They'll be quite impressed that you've taken the initiative. Again, your main task is to listen and learn. Let them do most of the talking.

Find out what they envisage your role to be. Drop in the odd comment to show that you've actually done some research into the industry. That'll convince them that you are serious about wanting to learn. Mention any areas which you've found particularly interesting. This will sow a seed in the minds of both colleagues and managers that you want to be involved and to contribute. By the time you start work, if they haven't decided what your role will be, they soon will.

Time For Action

One problem you'll be up against is time. No one has the time (some don't even have the inclination) to show you how to do things. Don't get disheartened if you're not given much to do – it's usually just because people think it will be easier and quicker to do things themselves than to have to teach you.

At this time, it is imperative that you let your manager and colleagues know your areas of expertise and your strengths (we'll discuss those later in this chapter, don't worry). This doesn't mean that you start blowing your own trumpet in the middle of the office, but if everyone seems to be spending a lot of time analyzing figures on their computers, and you have a passion for spreadsheets, SPEAK UP. Offer to at least help with inputting data.

Once someone agrees to let you try, there are only two rules :

1) Beat the agreed deadline, and

2) Check your work at least three times. If it's inaccurate, you'll have an almost impossible task convincing them to let you 'help' in the future.

If you follow these tips when you're starting out, we might finally break the usual pattern of people being frustrated at work. Of course, when you get to the top, remember what it was like when you started, and make things better for the next generation of freshers.

'Don't tell me how hard you work, tell me how much you achieve.'

We are often dissatisfied and frustrated with our work, because we can't see how to make things better, and feel like we're condemned for life. You could be following your job description to the letter, going beyond the call of duty, using your initiative, or be the most popular person in your department, and yet at the end of the year, when you ask for a payrise, you get a rude awakening.

What you might have failed to recognize was that the extra work you've been doing is not really useful to anyone, people interpret your working late as a sign that you can't cope, and the main reason you're popular is because no one thinks you're good enough to be a threat to them or their jobs.

When We're So Good They Hate Us

The other side of the coin is that you're not very popular. Assuming you're not a colleague from hell who spoils everyone's day, it may be that others see how bright you are, and the potential you have, and therefore are scared that you'll show up their inadequacies or maybe even take their jobs.

An ideal manager will be able to read these situations and assess you on your abilities. Few of us however, work for ideal managers. Instead, many of us work for supervisors or managers who are scared that we might take their jobs, who think of us as another piece of machinery/equipment, or who only

have us in their team as a status symbol. (In some organizations, the more members of staff a person manages, the more
important they feel.)

Value Added Titbits

Employers hope for more from their employees than most of
us realize. The sort of things which seemed so important at
school, like being punctual and finishing our work on time,
are not enough. They want us to *contribute*. In this context, to
contribute is to add extra value to the company, often by saving it money, becoming more efficient, or developing staff. It's
using our initiative to find ways to constantly improve things.

What do I mean by 'Using our initiative'? I mean doing
things we haven't been asked to do, but that we can see need
doing, or that will benefit the company. If you're one of the
millions who feels unappreciated and frustrated, chances are
you're doing enough to get by but not enough to stand out.

The trouble is, managers don't tell us that that's what they
want, which can mean that some dedicated workers will
spend their lives wondering why their commitment is not
being rewarded. Anyone can be a jobsworth, doing everything by the book, or just doing what's written in their contracts. And if you're happy to be like this, then obviously, you
won't be sacked. You might however be in the firing line if the
redundancy bell rings. The truth of the matter is, you're two a
penny. Even if you don't want to go the extra mile, at least
lighten up and be more flexible. Believe me, your customers
and colleagues will love you more for it, and that in itself will
increase your enjoyment and satisfaction.

For those of us who want to get a gold star or two, we have

to start using our imagination. Managers are looking for new ideas, new ways of making or saving money, or new ways to make clients happy. When we find answers to the following three questions, we'll be well on the way to success.

1) What stops me getting more done at work?

....

....

....

....

2) How can I cut down the time-consuming tasks?

....

....

....

....

3) What would I do to make my team/department more efficient if I was in charge?

....

....

....

....

To be considered a real special cookie, we've got to be able to motivate. Even being a specialist isn't as unique as the ability to get a group of people excited about doing their work. If you're good at motivating people in your personal life (sports team, kids, community group), work out what it is you're doing that gets them enthusiastic, and then use the same principle at work.

The Organizational Jigsaw

Not knowing how we fit into the great scheme of things can make us almost hate our jobs. None of us like the idea of being just another number on the payroll, doing a thankless task.

The worst example I ever heard about was a study done in a factory with some workers on a production line. Each person simply fitted two parts together for eight hours a day, as they passed on a conveyor belt. The people at the start of the line thought they were making radios, and the people halfway along thought they were making stereos. In fact, they were making TVs. How much satisfaction can a person feel when they don't even know what they're making?! The story does have a happy ending – the manager redesigned the production line, so that it was in the shape of a horseshoe. That meant that those at the start could see the end result. Productivity increased overnight. (What a surprise!!)

Now I'm not suggesting that *you* don't know what your department or company makes. But do you know how much your work contributes to company profits? (Or how much you cost?)

What Are You Worth?

In most organizations, the only ones who have an idea of what they're worth to the company are the salespeople. Lots of time is spent setting their goals, and calculating their bonuses if they over-perform. What about the rest of us?

How can a secretary, cleaner or cashier know what they're worth? For some reason, personnel specialists have traditionally divided us into two camps: The salespeople and senior managers, who get clear, measurable targets every month/ year, and us little people, who are supposed to make do with something general. Perhaps someone ought to tell them that little people need goals to get motivated too. Rather than wait for the penny to drop, there are a few things we can do ourselves.

Using your answers from the previous questionnaire, set yourself a target for the end of the month on one thing you're going to improve. Make it something that can be seen or measured, if possible.

As job satisfaction includes being praised, rewarded or at least noticed when you've done something good, talk to your boss. Let him know what you're planning and how it will benefit the company. Then work like hell to make sure you beat your target. If for some reason your boss isn't impressed, or doesn't bother to say 'well done', don't get frustrated. Simply tell other people. Pretty soon, other managers will hear how you've saved your department tons of money, and they'll come and ask you to tell them how you did it. They might even offer you a job with them. If nothing else, your manager might wake up to the fact that he has a star in his team.

Finally, speak to your boss/personnel manager, and ask if you can have goals set in the same way the directors/salestaff do. Make some suggestions of what could be included for your job, and then see what they come up with for the whole organization. (If they say it's impractical, remind them of the last time-saving thing you achieved, and the fact that you could have been assessed on that.)

Everyone Can Be More Efficient

Some of you might be feeling left out, because you don't do the sort of work which is easily measured. Don't despair! Whether you're an air steward, builder, chef or insurance rep, you can still take the initiative, using the same principle:

1) Pick one aspect of your job, however small, that you think could be done better.

2) When you've found a way to become more efficient, work out how much time you've saved in a month.

3) To really impress, you can find out from your boss how many others in your company are doing a similar job. Then you know how many work hours your idea could save the whole organization.

4) Finally, calculate how much you're paid an hour (before tax), and multiply this by the number of hours saved, and the number of people who could also benefit.

So you see, that half an hour you save by making one less trip up and down the stairs every day, can add up to 100 hours a month if there are 10 of you who do the same thing. If you each earn around £5 an hour, that's £500 a month you've saved. Not only that, but the extra half hour you now have each day, can be used to make/save the company even more money.

Reap The Benefits

Of course you should be rewarded for your efforts, just like salespeople are. Maybe you can make a deal in advance with your boss: If you find a way to save the company £500 a month, will he arrange for you to get a bonus of £100? Will he put you forward for promotion? Will he at least buy you a bottle of your favourite tipple, and get you mentioned in the company newsletter?

Let's imagine you can't do a deal with your boss, but you can think of a couple of ways to save the company money. What do you do? First you decide which job you'd like to be doing next. Which department do you want to be in ? Which manager would you like to work for? What areas of responsibility would you like?

Choose the money-saving idea which you think is most relevant to the next job you want. One that should impress your next manager. Then, when you've shown what a star you are by being so efficient, you mention it to the boss you'd like to work for. Don't forget to mention the job you'd like to do next. (Too often people don't ask for what they want, and just hope that somehow they'll get it anyway.) You may have to do this more than once, but eventually they'll see you're good as well as keen, and then will bear you in mind when a vacancy arises.

Meanwhile, you should be enjoying your work a bit more, because you'll be setting and achieving real targets. Naturally, you can also mention these achievements when it's time for your next pay review.

The Importance Of Fun

The last few sections have been based on the assumption that you're dissatisfied with your job because you want more recognition, responsibility, or promotion. In these circumstances you need to show the people who make decisions that you are good enough to do a higher paid, more responsible job, before they even let you try.

But what if you don't particularly want the extra headache that will come with another job? What if all you really want is to enjoy your work a bit more? Nothing wrong with that – most companies know that happy workers are better workers. And the happier you are at work, the less stressed out you'll be when you get home.

There are hundreds of little things you can do each day to make your work more rewarding and enjoyable. Here's a list of 10 to get your imagination working:

1) Smile at people: customers, colleagues and bosses will all respond to you more positively.

2) Organize monthly socials for your team – anything from a few drinks to a night at the theatre.

3) Set yourself a challenge of not saying anything negative before 10am.(Start the day right, and it'll only get better.)

4) If you use a computer, set it up to have a funny message every time you switch it on.

5) Brighten up your workspace with flowers, a bowl of fruit, or pictures.

6) Set yourself hourly/daily goals with a small reward if you achieve them. (e.g. if you type 10 letters before lunch, you can have your favourite dessert.)

7) Start a competition with your colleagues for the funniest/ strangest thing a customer says to you each day.

8) Keep a supply of your favourite sweets/fruit handy, and only allow yourself one when you've pleased a customer, or done something well.

9) The hour after lunch is often called the graveyard slot, because everyone's energy levels are so low. So arrange to do your favourite task immediately after lunch. (Also, do your least favourite task first, so you haven't got it hanging over you.)

10) Pick an item from the previous day's news which each of you has to make up a joke about. Best joke gets a drink/newspaper/ice-cream etc.

I'm sure you'll think of much better ways to stay amused, but these will at least brighten up the day a little.

Playing To Your Strengths

I didn't fully appreciate the importance of job satisfaction until I started looking into self-employment options. Then, I chose to take the time to analyze my strengths, skills, and hobbies, to see what type of work I'd enjoy most. Not only that, I analysed what I'd loved or hated about my previous jobs.

For example, I am a communicator – speaking, writing, instructing all give me a buzz. For months in my last job, however, I was asked to sit in front of a computer for eight hours a day, analyzing the European oil market. I was then meant to send out a summary of my analysis to all the sales teams. BOREDOM CITY! To try to liven things up a bit, I'd put little fun messages in with the figures. Although the figures were correct, this didn't go down well at all. Oil prices were a serious issue, and I had no business trying to make them more interesting.

When I was younger, I worked in a clothes shop, as a 'Saturday Girl'. All I had to do was put clothes on the rails and occasionally answer any customer queries. The highlight of my day was when I was put on Fitting Room duty, just because I had more opportunity to talk to the customers.

So when I was choosing what I wanted to be, I looked at all the work I'd ever done, from working in a clothes shop on a Saturday, to working as a care assistant in a home for the elderly and mentally infirm. I even considered the cleaning jobs I'd had. After making a list of what I enjoyed about them all, and what I hated most, I went on to look at my personal life, my hobbies and interests. Finally, I made a list of things I knew I was good at. The result was my company, 21st Century

Training. Even though I now often work 10–12 hour days, I've never been so happy in all my life. That's why I want you to go through the same exercises. Whether you want to be self-employed or not, it's still important to be doing something you enjoy and are good at.

SKILLS AND STRENGTHS CHECK LIST

When completing the following , please include unpaid work too:

1) PRACTICAL SKILLS e.g. typing, gardening, cooking, repairs etc.

....

....

....

2) ARTISTIC SKILLS e.g. music, dance, painting, writing etc.

....

....

....

3) INTELLECTUAL SKILLS e.g. problem solving, new ideas, understanding, numerical.

....

....

....

4) ACTIVITY SKILLS e.g. sport, camping, keep fit, cycling.

    ....

    ....

    ....

5) LEISURE TIME e.g. reading, clubs, concerts, voluntary
    work.

    ....

    ....

    ....

6) SOCIAL STRENGTHS e.g. making friends, helping people,
    making people laugh.

    ....

    ....

    ....

7) PERSONAL STRENGTHS e.g. honesty, patience, energetic,
    generous, caring.

    ....

    ....

    ....

Using My Strengths

Hopefully, you now have a long list of things you're good at,
and things you enjoy. The next step is to go back and put a tick
by all of those you currently use at work. (For those not working, put a tick by all those you would like to use in your next
job.)

I'm no careers guidance counsellor, but my bet is that if you're not using more than half of your strengths and skills, you'll be frustrated. I know I was. Now what? Well, we have three choices:

A) Find a way to use more of our skills in our current jobs

B) Find a job which gives us a chance to use more of our strengths

C) Find a way to make money out of our skills and strengths e.g. self-employment.

Strictly speaking, there is a fourth choice – we could ignore everything we've written down, and choose to remain frustrated and depressed. But I know you want more than that, don't you?

As a first step, you can start looking at job ads, and scoring them against how many of your skills you could use doing the job. This might help you to decide what you'd rather be doing, if you're not sure. Talk to people who do the sort of work you're interested in. Find out what it's really like. If you don't know anyone, write to companies for more information. Go to a careers adviser – your local job centre will tell you how to get free advice.

Don't forget to talk to your boss. Chances are she doesn't even realize you're so talented. Ask what jobs in the organization they think would give you the opportunity to use your skills. Then ask her advice on what you need to be ready to apply.

If you are considering self-employment (and even if you're

not) read the money chapter, and decide a plan of action.

Whatever you decide, make it your decision. Don't make the mistakes so many of us do, of getting a job which will impress others, but bore us to tears, or worse, just taking anything that's offered. Believe me, in the long run, you'll regret it.

> *There's no labour a man can do that's undignified,*
> *if he does it right.*
>
> BILL COSBY

CHAPTER FIVE

I Want More . . . Confidence

*The greatest pleasure in life, is doing what people
say you cannot do*

WALTER BAGEHOT (1826–77)

I know someone, who, at 22 has had a TV programme made
about her, just finished a degree at London School of
Economics, and is already running her own PR company,
with clients like Chris Eubank and Chrystal Rose.

Some people who watched the programme thought she was
arrogant. Others thought she was a pain in the ass. I thought
she was brilliant. Why the difference of opinion? Because I celebrate when I see anyone who is confident enough to say 'I'm
pretty, I'm intelligent, and I'm going to make a lot of money'.

Shaa is half American. Maybe that's why she can look anyone straight in the eye, and tell them these things, as if she
were telling them the time.

British False Modesty

What about us Brits? We think it's bad taste to sing our own
praises, or 'blow our own trumpets.' We prefer the subtle
approach – false modesty, understatement, and waiting
patiently for other people to recognize our talents.

Let's do a quick exercise. I want you to write down the first words which come into your head, when you think of each of the following people:

Madonna	....
Richard Branson	....
Muhammed Ali	....
Joan Collins	....

What do these people have in common ? No, Besides enormous amounts of money? They all had the confidence to let others know how good they were at what they do/did.

How often do we watch someone on TV and think 'Boy, I could do better than that'? So how come we're still catching the bus, and they're riding around in limos?

It's not necessarily the best people who succeed in this world (though it does help to have some talent), it's the ones who push themselves forward, the ones who grab every opportunity. While we sit thinking 'Oh I couldn't do that, what would people think?', others are getting on with it and saying 'Stuff what people think, they're not gonna pay my mortgage for me'.

Fear

If Nelson Mandela, Mahatma Ghandi, John F. Kennedy or even Einstein, had not bothered for fear of what people might say, we'd be living in a much worse world today. The point is, there's no difference between them and us: They might have been scared that people would laugh at them and their ideas, but they knew the secret which was the title of a book in the '80's: *Feel The Fear & Do It Anyway.*

Having confidence and courage doesn't mean having no

fear, just accepting that it's worth a few butterflies to change the world!! Everyone is scared sometimes. Whether it's walking into a room of strangers, speaking in public, going for an interview, or telling someone to get lost, the symptoms are the same. You know, dry mouth, sweaty palms, churning stomach, trembling legs etc. Unfortunately, most of us let our fears control our lives, and therefore how little we achieve.

Acting As If

I don't believe there is such a thing as a 'naturally confident' person. There are those who let their fear stop them, and those who don't. Most people would describe me as confident, not realizing that half the time I'm operating on the 'Act As If' principle. When I have to go into a situation I've never been in before, or have to do something I'm scared about, I go through a set procedure you might find useful:

1) I play the music I usually play when I'm celebrating successes.

2) I put on my most knock-'em-dead outfit.

3) I throw my shoulders back, hold my head up, and walk like I own the street.

4) I keep picturing in my mind everything going so brilliantly that I get a standing ovation.

That, in a nutshell, is the 'act as if' principle. You ask yourself how you would look, and act if you were totally confident, then just do it.

To start with, you'll probably be as sceptical as I was, but believe me, it works. Our brains take their cue from our bodies. If we smile, our brains register that we must be happy, so they start making our muscles relax. If we walk with our eyes fixed on the ground, our brains will register that we're depressed or feeling unconfident.

This little trick can be used when going for an interview, at a party, when asking for a refund in a shop, or even when asking for a payrise.

Over-Confident

I'm forever hearing people describe others as 'over-confident', meaning 'too big for his boots' or 'riding for a fall'. Get outta my face! When someone says a person is over-confident, what they mean is that person is more confident than them, or as confident as they would like to be.

Perhaps I should explain what I mean when I say 'confident'. I'm not talking about showing off, kidding yourself into believing you're something you're not, or thinking that you're better than others. All these are just signs that you're a sad or annoying individual.

What Is Confidence?

1) Believing I'm As Good As Anyone Else.

Many of us feel that if someone has more qualifications/more experience/a slimmer body/more money/more knowledge etc then that makes them better than us. Total B.S.

Just because a man has a degree, doesn't mean he has any

common sense, or would know how to re-wire a house. A rich woman might have such a bitchy personality that no one likes her. A politician might quote statistics, but couldn't mend a fan-belt or give a decent haircut. The point is that no one is better than anyone else. We're all good at different things. When we feel inferior, it's just because the other person is 'playing at home' so to speak. i.e. they're talking about their favourite subject. If we want to balance things up again, we simply turn the tables, and talk about our areas of expertise, whether that's bringing up children or playing pool.

Einstein said that imagination was more important than knowledge, and you can't tell me you don't have an imagination.

2) Being Aware Of Skills I Have Which Are Better
Than Average.

There's a big difference between thinking you're better than someone else, and realizing that you're *better at* something than somebody else. In the first case, you're saying that the other person doesn't deserve the same respect, and in the second, you're saying that you have developed different skills to them.

One of my skills is communication. I've presented in front of audiences and had standing ovations. Sometimes, people come up to me after a seminar, and say they wish they could present like me. Although it's very flattering (and boy, am I a sucker for a compliment), I try to find out what they're good at, to remind them that I'm not better, just different.

In the job satisfaction chapter, I asked you to list your skills and strengths. I once told my mate Eve to do the same thing, when she was particularly fed up with her job. To start with, she didn't know what to write down, but with a little prompting, the woman filled two pages!

We all have different talents and hobbies, and the things we enjoy, we do most often. Naturally, practice makes improvement (perfection is a myth), so each of us becomes good at stuff we like. Who are we to judge whether being good at football is better than being good at maths? Or being good at listening is better than being good at plumbing? 'Vive la difference', that's what I say. (For those of you who didn't enjoy French at school, it means roughly, 'hurray, and long live differences'.)

I'm as wow-ed by Linford Christie sprinting, as I am by my friend Janet's dressmaking or my brother's chessplaying. But I don't get insecure, because I know there are things I can do better than them. Next time you see somebody doing something that you're not very good at, think how useless they would be doing your job, or something you're brilliant at.

3) Remembering My Successes & Not Dwelling On My Failures.

How many of you have had a triple F in an exam? Oh, just me then. Well I never wanted to be an accountant anyway. What about driving tests – I didn't just fail three times, I had to go one better: The first time I took my test, I didn't notice the stop sign and white lines across the side road I was coming out of, so I joined a dual carriageway at 40 mph. Needless to say, the examiner used his emergency brake, which automatically means you've failed. Not wanting to waste my time, I got out of the car, and caught the bus home, leaving examiner and car where we stopped. It was over a year before I dared to even book another lesson.

When I finally did pass (fourth attempt), it was because I'd stopped thinking about the first failure, and started to think about reasons why I should pass. I'd done everything right in my last few lessons, so I pretended that this was just another one, but with a new instructor. Every time he told me to make a manoeuvre, I took my time, thought through exactly how I'd done it in the last lesson, and then did the same.

Nowadays, it's not trendy to use the word 'failure', as it's too negative. Instead, we should all be talking about 'feedback'. When something doesn't go according to plan, as long as we learn from it, it's not failure. But how many of us *do* learn from the past? Isn't it much more common for us to dwell on all the terrible mistakes we've made, and vow never to even try again?

Is it any wonder that we're scared to try new things, if every time we're about to start, we think of the last time something went wrong? Not only that, but our nearest and dearest will chip in and remind us of the bad times too. (I know they only do it because they don't want us to be hurt/rejected, but there comes a time when we have to remind them that we're old enough to cope, whatever the outcome.)

It's funny how selective we are about which failures we remember: do you remember how many times you tried to stand up/walk as a child and fell down? Did your mother tell you not to bother, because you might hurt yourself again, or did she encourage you, and make you feel it was OK to fail?

As soon as we're successful at something, we hardly remember all the failure, pain and embarrassment that got us there. So next time you're faced with a difficult or new experience, think about one you had years ago, which turned out OK and tell yourself there's no reason why this won't too.

Forget what other people might think if you mess up. *The only failure is in no longer trying.*

4) Accepting That I'm Only Human and Therefore I Will Make Mistakes.

There are things I've done in my life which I don't so much regret as I cringe to think about. Anyone who's past their teenage years will know exactly what I mean.

At school, we're given the impression that making a mistake makes us less of a person. It's taken me years to realize that making mistakes makes us more human. You'd all be bored stiff, and have thrown this book in the bin by now, if all I'd written about were all the sensible, wise and successful things I've done. (Admittedly, the book would have been a lot shorter too!).

It's amazing how easily we forgive and forget when our loved ones screw up, but cling on to the memories when it's us who've got it wrong. Eventually, though, we have to accept that these things happened, they're in the past, and although we may not be proud of what we did, we're not gonna spend our lives apologizing. I don't often use religious references, but there is one that is very apt.

In the days when Jews used to stone serious sinners (i.e. throw rocks at them until they were dead), Jesus was trying to make a point about no one being perfect, and therefore no one being in a position to judge the behaviour of others. All he said was: 'Let he who is without sin, cast the first stone.'

This isn't to say that we just go around willy-nilly breaking the rules, and being evil, cause no one's in a position to judge. What I'm saying is we'd do well to remember that part of being human involves making mistakes. There isn't a damned thing we can do about it. If we don't make mistakes, we don't learn, we don't advance, and we never become the sort of people we want to be.

It's a sad fact that there are still thousands of bosses out there who punish people for making mistakes. How else do they expect them to learn? How else do they expect them to come up with ideas on how to make the company more successful? If you were anything like me, you didn't listen to all the wise words your parents said. You only learnt when you went out there and made the mistakes for yourself. Going to school doesn't teach us half of what we need to know to survive as adults. Trying things out (and making mistakes) does.

5) Realizing That I Should Welcome Both Compliments and Constructive Criticism.

Genuine compliments are all too rare these days. The reason I know this is because of the look on people's faces when I pay them one. They don't know what to say or how to react, so they end up throwing it back in my face (unintentionally, of course). When I say they throw it back in my face, I mean they don't accept it. Let me give you an example:

'Hey your dress looks beautiful!'

'What, this old thing? I've had it ages'

or

'You're brilliant with that computer '

'Oh, it's nothing, anyone could do it'

Did I ask how long she'd had the dress? Is she saying I have no taste because I think something old looks beautiful? What about our computer friend? Is he making out I'm a dork because any sensible person could be as good as him?

What's wrong with a simple 'thank you', that's what I want to know. Apparently, if we thank someone for a compliment, it could sound as though we're agreeing with them. And we can't have that, can we?! Heaven forbid that we should actually think something good about ourselves! What few of us seem to realize is, while we're busy being humble, we're hurting the other person's feelings. We might as well smack them in the mouth, or say 'stuff your compliment'.

We're all wise enough to suss out the sly foxes who try to pay us compliments so that we'll do something for them. Kids are the worst culprits. They think they can hide their ulterior motives behind those innocent smiles. But if we just take a compliment at face value, no one can trick us into anything. After all, a compliment is just a positive comment about you. So smile, say thank you, and walk a little taller.

Criticism isn't so easy for most of us to handle. We tend to assume that criticism is always negative, when often, people are trying to help us. An easy way to work out whether someone is giving constructive criticism, or just being wicked, is to stay calm, and ask them why they think what they do. If they can explain their comments rationally, chances are you'll end up thanking them for caring. If they rant and rave, or can't back up their argument, tell them to take a hike. The difference between being an arrogant fool, and a wise, confident person, is often the ability to accept criticism, and act on it.

Although I didn't fully appreciate it at the time, and felt picked on, if Miss Mead, my first English teacher hadn't criticized my Bristolian English, I'd never be able to do the job I do now, or even write a book you could all understand. Now, I communicate with confidence. Then, I felt intimidated by people who used long words, or who never dropped their t's and h's.

6) Being In Control Of My Emotions, and Remembering That I Choose My Moods.

Confident people don't seem to lose their cool as much as some of us do, or at least, not in public. They cope. How? By staying calm, and doing some of the things we've already discussed. When a person chooses to remember how many times they've coped before, not how many times they've failed, they feel sure that they'll manage their latest crisis.

By the same token, when a person believes they're as good as everyone else, they aren't fazed by anyone who tries to make them look small. Think of the last time you got upset or angry in public, and later regretted it. What thoughts went through your mind? You probably don't remember word for word, but let me try my telepathic trick, and see if I can pick your brains.

Chances are, you reminded yourself of all the horrible things the person you were angry with, ever did to you. (Dragging up the past is the oldest trick in the book.) Then you probably tried to hurt them with some vicious comment they didn't deserve. Lastly, you may have really pushed the boat out, and washed your dirty linen in public. Am I on the right track? (If I'm not, you're either a saint, or already in control of your emotions.)

For those of us with fallen halos, we never seem to break the cycle. Every time we feel hurt or let down, we lash out, doing even more damage in the process. Why? Because it's easier to do that than to maintain self-control, and talk rationally. To be a confident person, we have to believe that we can control our emotions and reactions. We have to believe that people will listen to us if we talk quietly.

It takes guts to face a hurtful situation calmly. It takes courage to overcome our fear that someone will take advantage, if we bear our souls to them instead of retaliating. But that's exactly what we need to do. Next time you're having a bad experience with someone, and you're about to shout something hurtful, stop yourself. The old count to ten routine really does work. Then wait until you're alone, and talk to them about how they hurt your feelings. Explain why you felt the way you did, and what you'd rather they did next time. Believe me, you'll respect yourself a lot more this way, and that in turn will boost your confidence.

7) Putting My Happiness First, While Trying Not To Hurt Anyone Else.

What's the point in living, if we're not doing things which make us happy? (That's not a cue for anyone to release any suicidal tendencies, it's a cue for everyone to start putting themselves first.) Somewhere along the line, we've changed the rules of the game, and made selfishness a really bad thing. Well, it's time to rip up the rulebooks and party. Mamma Myers is here to tell you that selfishness is natural. Before I get angry letters from socialists, and those with religious faith, I'd better explain.

Our first priority must be to take care of ourselves, otherwise, we'll be in no position to help others even if we want to. How can a parent who doesn't exercise be fit enough to play with his kids as much as they'd like? How can a woman with no social life be stimulating or fun to work for? How can we donate to charity if we don't have a job of our own?

It's only by being selfish that human beings have survived so long. There is nothing wrong with putting your own happiness and well-being first, as long as you try not to hurt others in the process. When we're happy, we're more fun to live with, more fun to work with, and more fun to be with.

When we stop feeling guilty for having fun, we become more relaxed and confident. Haven't you noticed how much confident people smile? That's not just coincidence – they put as much effort into their enjoyment as they do into their work. In the same way we understand the need to put work before pleasure, we need to learn the importance of putting our happiness before everyone else's. If we don't, we're on the road to nervous breakdown, depression, or worse.

You know you're a confident person when you can refuse to join in with something which makes you unhappy, or insist on doing something simply because it makes you happy. This can be hard for those of us who have always put other people first, so we need to start small.

We can make a deal with ourselves that for every time we put someone else first, we'll do something afterwards which we enjoy, and not feel guilty about it. Next, we can plan a reward for every time we stand up for ourselves. So for example, each time we have the guts to say 'No, I don't want to do that, I'm going to do this instead', we allow ourselves a little treat.

Naturally, your nearest and dearest will be freaked out, and accuse you of not loving them any more because you're not the doormat they know and abuse. Be prepared for serious guilt trips. If the guilt gets too much for you, offer a compromise. But the ideal is to get to the stage where you can say what you feel. Tell them you love them heaps, but you love yourself too, and then carry on.

Unless you can give me 20 good reasons why your happiness isn't as important as everyone else's, I want you to promise to at least try. Deal?

8) Knowing I am Loved By People Who Know Me Well.

When we lack confidence, we tend to wallow in self-pity, and pretend that nobody loves us. This then becomes a vicious circle. We tell ourselves nobody loves us, then we 'reason' that this must be because there's something wrong with us, then we think 'What's the point in trying to talk to people, they won't like me anyway?'

If we haven't crawled into a cupboard to hide from the world at this stage, we might pig out on fattening food, get drunk, take drugs, or all three. Now for the real killer – we then tell ourselves nobody likes us because we're fat, drunk, or junkies. And what do we do when we feel unloved? Yep, we eat more fattening food, drink even more, and take even stronger drugs. I can't be the only one who sees a flaw in this argument.

Allow me to try to break your vicious circle. I know it's served you well, and I'm no qualified counsellor or psychiatrist, but it can't hurt to let me try. (If I don't succeed, please do see one of the aforementioned; you don't realize how many of us out here want to get to know you, and love you.)

Let's start with the first link in the chain – nobody loves you. Is this strictly true? If you made a list of every human being who knows you, could you honestly say that not one of them thought you were an OK person? If you can think of even one person who cares about you, then chances are there are others you don't realize, who do. Even if there aren't any others, you must be doing something right for this person to think you're worth caring about.

Right, we've established that you are potentially loveable. What may have happened is that you've met more than your fair share of bogeys in life – people who treated you badly, and who convinced you that you were the one with a problem. No sir-ee, sonny Jim, they're the ones who need therapy! You just need to meet a few decent people you can trust.

Spend more time with those on your list who you feel actually do care about you. Ask them to introduce you to *their* friends or family, and slowly build up a group of friends of your own, who love you just as you are. Once you see that more than one person thinks you're special, you'll start to feel confident, knowing that there's nothing wrong with you after all.

If you really can't think of anyone who likes you, can you think of any reasons why the people who don't like you feel that way? I want serious, concrete reasons, not the silly excuses you use to justify your self-pity.

Are you insulting? Do you smell? Have you hurt their feelings? Once you work out the exact reason (and if you can't work it out, ask), then you can do something about it, so that you won't upset people in the future. As for those who you've already upset , maybe an apology plus a promise to try not to hurt them again could help. Make sense? Worth a try?

Don't forget that this is a two-way street. While you're gaining confidence from realizing people like you, you'll be helping others to feel more confident, just by liking them, I know you're a little gem, so go on out there and shine!

9) Making The Most Of My Good Points.

There is often an impression that confident people are the most attractive ones in society. I'd say it was the other way around: when people start making the most of their good points, and playing down their faults, they become more confident and therefore more attractive.

Nobody's perfect, and even those who are paid millions for looking good are often not totally happy with their appearance. A lot of being confident comes from choosing what to focus on. We can either concentrate on the best or the worst of anything.

A very good friend of mine (you know who you are Kathryn), has the most amazing legs a woman could hope for. For years, I tried to persuade her to show them off, by wearing skirts which were just a little above the knee. Instead she'd moan about her stomach being too large (could hardly see it), or her hair not being how she wanted it to be. In the last couple of years, she has had admirers declaring their undying love, she's gone from being shy and avoiding risks, to bungee jumping, making heaps of friends, and even travelling abroad alone. Now I'm not saying it is only because she started wearing clothes which emphasized her best points, but I do think it helped. When she stopped worrying about what she thought wasn't perfect, she realized that no one else even noticed the things she used to worry about.

I went shopping with a male friend of mine a while ago, and chose some outfits which I thought emphasized his best points, while staying in keeping with his personality. He couldn't believe how many compliments he got. I smiled as I watched his self-confidence soar through the roof.

What are your best features? Don't tell me you don't have

any – everyone does. If you really can't think of any, talk to your best friend/mother/partner/sister etc. Next time you need new clothes, take them with you, and make a day of it. Promise yourself you won't just plump for the same styles you've been wearing since 1983. And whatever you do, don't plump for the cheapest. Buy fewer things of higher quality. They hang better, look better, last longer, and make you feel better. Dare to look good, and wait for the compliments to flow. (Don't forget, when they do, just say thank you, smile, and walk a little taller.)

10) Understanding That One Person's Success Doesn't Mean My Failure.

Most of us are confident at least some of the time. What happens is that we see someone achieving more than us, or getting where we want to be before us, and it all goes out of the window. Suddenly we become mere shadows of our former selves. Somehow, we manage to convince ourselves that their success is our failure. No way José. Not so Billy Jo.

If we're not careful, we can become bitter, twisted, jealous individuals, finding reasons why it's not fair that someone is doing 'better' than us. Then we spend so much time worrying about their good luck, and our bad, that we stop even trying to achieve what we originally set out to.

Whether we're comparing ourselves with someone at work, on the TV, or down the road, we start believing that they achieved their success at our expense. Where's the law which says there can only be one good hairdresser/builder/director or sales manager in your part of the world?

The constructive, rewarding way to deal with these situations, is to draw up an action plan for achieving what you want and stick to it. If possible, find out what others have done. Learn from their mistakes, and save yourself some time, money and heartache.

Regardless of how many others are ahead of you, don't give up. I once read that 'Success basically means to persevere'. Some of those who appear to be doing better than you at the moment, will give up, get lazy, retire or burn out. As long as you're still trying, there's every chance that you can overtake them.

Not being the first, doesn't mean you're not one of the best. If you can picture yourself being successful, and you keep working towards your goal, with that picture in mind, you'll get there. Stop worrying, get out there, and kick ass!

Re-Defining Con-Artists

Confidence has had a bad press because of the con-men and women we hear about, who seem to be forever ripping off grannies and poor people. It's got to the stage where if someone sounds confident, we're automatically suspicious of them. Madness! Personally, I think people who pretend not to be as good as they really are, are the ones to be suspicious about.

Before I leave this topic, I want to make sure I haven't lost any of you on the way. So far, you've had an easy ride compared to the other chapters; all you've had to do is sit back and read. But, true to form, I've designed a little bit of homework for you. It won't take long, but it could make a big difference to your lives.

Switch on your memory and imagination buttons, we're going down forgotten territory. Is everybody ready? Then let's go.

Three things I've been complimented on:

....
....
....

Three things I know I'm good at:

....
....
....

Three things I've done successfully:

....
....
....

Three criticisms I've found to be useful:

....
....
....

Three people who care about me:

....
....
....

Three of my best features:

....
....
....

Three things I would like to try:

....
....
....

Three reasons why I haven't yet:

....
....
....

Three things I'll feel if I do try:

....
....
....

Three people who will help me if I do try:

....
....
....

Three actions I'm going to take this week:

....
....
....

And Finally,
Three ways I'm going to celebrate when I succeed:

....
....
....

Instead of finishing with a short quote, I'm going to give you my favourite poem, author unknown, which I recite at most of the presentations I ever deliver. Hope you like it.

IT'S ALL IN THE STATE OF MIND

If you think you're beaten, you are
If you think you dare not, you don't.
If you'd like to win, but think you can't,
It's almost certain you won't.
If you think you'll lose, you've lost.
For in this world we find
Success begins with a person's will
It's all in the state of mind.
If you think you're outclassed, you are -
You've got to think high to rise
You've got to be sure of yourself
Before you can ever win the prize.
Life's battles don't always go
To the stronger or faster man.
But sooner or later, the person who wins,
Is the person who <u>thinks</u> they can.

Grand Finale

Well, that's all folks, as they say. OK not quite all: I didn't write this book just to try to get rich. I meant what I said in the introduction – I want ordinary people to see that they can make things better, they can make a difference. As a firm believer in putting your money where your mouth is, I've decided it's . . .

COMPETITION TIME!

There will be one winner for each of the five categories (Love, Money, Job Satisfaction, Respect and Confidence). All I want you to do, is to write to me (1 side of A4) at the address below, in a few months' time, telling me how you've applied something you read in this book to improve some area of your life.

The deadline for applications will be 30 June 1996, so you have plenty of time. Each winner will receive a cheque for £200, a weekend at the Savoy for two, and a free place on one of my training courses. Send applications to me

c/o Twenty-First Century Training,
Coppergate House,
16 Brune Street,
London E1 7NJ

I look forward to hearing about your achievements.
Success and Happiness To You All!